Ireland

Ireland

BY JEAN F. BLASHFIELD

Enchantment of the World™
Second Series

CHILDREN'S PRESS®

An Imprint of Scholastic Inc.

New York   Toronto   London   Auckland   Sydney
Mexico City   New Delhi   Hong Kong
Danbury, Connecticut

Frontispiece: **Cliffs of Moher**

Consultant: Mike Cronin, Academic Director, Boston College–Ireland, Dublin

Please note: All statistics are as up-to-date as possible at the time of publication.

Book production by The Design Lab

Library of Congress Cataloging-in-Publication Data
Blashfield, Jean F.
  Ireland / by Jean F. Blashfield.—[Revised edition].
      pages cm.—(Enchantment of the world—second series)
  Includes bibliographical references and index.
  ISBN 978-0-531-23676-5 (lib. bdg.)
1. Ireland—Juvenile literature. I. Title.
  DA906.B58 2013
  941.7—dc23   2013002015

1 2 3 4 5 6 7 8 9 10 R 23 22 21 20 19 18 17 16 15 14

Girl playing the fiddle

Contents

Left to right: **Trinity College Library, street signs, Irish Travellers, farmers, Galway**

CHAPTER 1

A Hundred Thousand Welcomes

RELAND IS A LAND OF DEEP GREEN FIELDS, DRAMATIC cliffs, and misty gray days. It is a place where eerie stone monuments built by ancient people still stand, and where fantastic legends were told by Celtic settlers 2,500 years ago. Today, Ireland is home to friendly people, lively music, vibrant cities, and thriving arts.

Ireland is both a nation and the island where that nation is located. The island of Ireland lies just to the west of the island of Great Britain, off the northwestern coast of Europe. The Republic of Ireland covers about five-sixths of the island of Ireland. The remainder of the island is a region called Northern Ireland, which, along with England, Scotland, and Wales, make up the United Kingdom. Ireland was divided in 1922, when it won its independence from Great Britain. Some Irish people hope that someday the republic and Northern Ireland will again be united. In the meantime, people can pass freely between the countries. Some people cross the border every day to go to work.

Opposite: **Dublin is famous for its Georgian architecture, a style popular in the 1700s. Many Georgian houses in Dublin feature elaborate door knockers.**

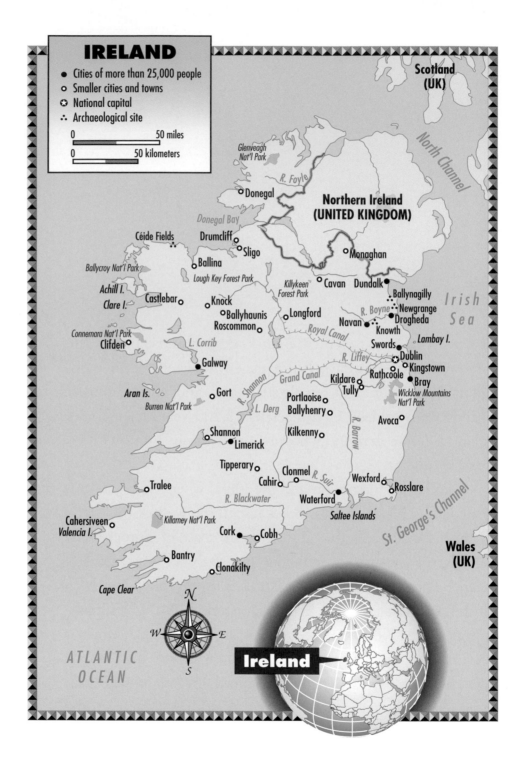

IRELAND

- ● Cities of more than 25,000 people
- ○ Smaller cities and towns
- ✪ National capital
- ∴ Archaeological site

0   50 miles

0   50 kilometers

Scotland (UK)

North Channel

Glenveagh Nat'l Park

○ Donegal

R. Foyle

Northern Ireland (UNITED KINGDOM)

Donegal Bay

Céide Fields ∴   Drumcliff ○

○ Sligo

○ Monaghan

Ballycroy Nat'l Park

○ Ballina

Lough Key Forest Park

Killykeen Forest Park

○ Cavan   Dundalk ●

● Ballynagilly

Irish Sea

Achill I.

Clare I.

Castlebar ○

○ Knock

○ Ballyhaunis

○ Longford

R. Boyne   ● Newgrange

Navan ●   ● Drogheda

Roscommon ○

Royal Canal

● Knowth

Connemara Nat'l Park

Clifden ○

L. Corrib

Lambay I.

Swords ●

R. Liffey

● Dublin ✪

● Galway

Grand Canal

Kingstown ○

Rathcoole ●   ● Bray

Aran Is.

○ Gort

Kildare ○

Tully ○

Wicklow Mountains Nat'l Park

R. Shannon

Burren Nat'l Park

○ Portlaoise

Ballyhenry ○

L. Derg

Avoca ○

Shannon ○   ● Limerick

Kilkenny ○

R. Barrow

Tipperary ○

Clonmel ○

R. Suir

Wexford ○

Cahir ○

Rosslare ○

● Tralee

● Waterford

R. Blackwater

Saltee Islands

St. George's Channel

Killarney Nat'l Park

Wales (UK)

Cahersiveen ○

Valencia I.

Cork ●   ○ Cobh

○ Bantry

○ Clonakilty

Cape Clear

N   W   E   S

ATLANTIC OCEAN

Ireland

Ireland is also a land of two languages. English is the most common language used, but Irish is also spoken. Irish is a Gaelic language, related to Scottish and Manx. It was the most common language spoken in Ireland until the nineteenth century. Today, about 2 percent of Irish people speak it in their everyday lives and about 42 percent of the people can speak it. Irish is the official first language of the country, so street signs and government titles and other official names are usually in Irish. The police force, for instance, is called the Gardaí, meaning "guardians."

A man reads an Irish-language newspaper in county Galway, in the west of Ireland.

Symbols of Ireland

The harp has been used as a symbol of Ireland for hundreds of years. Long ago, a harp player was at the center of social gatherings. The harp appeared in religious books in Ireland in the eighth century, possibly as a reference to the biblical King David, who played the harp. King James I of England placed the image of a harp on a flag as early as 1603. Soon thereafter, the yellow harp on a green background came to symbolize rebellion in Ireland. Today, it is a symbol of the Republic of Ireland and appears on all Irish coins.

The shamrock, a three-leafed clover, became associated with Ireland because tradition holds that St. Patrick, who spread Christianity in Ireland, explained the Trinity by using a clover. The Trinity is the Christian belief that God is three people in one: the father creator, the son Jesus Christ, and the holy spirit. There is no single plant called a shamrock; the word is used for a variety of plants with similarly shaped leaves. The name *shamrock* comes from the Irish *seamair óg*, meaning "young clover." Today, people associate the shamrock with Ireland, but it is not an official symbol.

The ancient Romans called Ireland Hibernia, which may have derived from words meaning "abundant land." But the Irish themselves take their name from a Celtic goddess named Ériu. The Irish word for Ireland is *Éireann* (pronounced AY-run).

Ireland has, at times, suffered from devastating famine and poverty. This has caused millions of Irish people to leave their home and try to make lives for themselves in other countries. Worldwide, at least seventy million people claim Irish ancestry. About half of those people live in the United States.

About four million people a year visit Ireland, which is almost as many people as live there. The Irish greet the visitors warmly. "*Céad míle fáilte*," they say, "a hundred thousand welcomes." Let's explore Ireland.

Cyclists ride through the rugged hills of county Mayo, in western Ireland.

CHAPTER 2

The Emerald Isle

TEN THOUSAND YEARS AGO, DURING THE LAST ICE age, the islands of Ireland and Great Britain were attached to the European mainland. Vast sheets of ice called glaciers covered the entire region. As the glaciers melted, the sea rose, flooding low-lying areas and creating these islands.

Shaped by Ice

The movement of the glaciers during the last ice age shaped many of the landforms found in Ireland today. The region called the drumlin belt is near the border with Northern Ireland. It features drumlins: low, teardrop-shaped hills made of rocky rubble. The pointed end of the teardrop lies to the north, the direction the ice was retreating as it melted. Because the drumlins are so rocky, this part of Ireland is not good for agriculture.

Eskers are formations that consist of ridges of sand and gravel. They are scattered across most of the island, but are most visible in the flat center of the country.

Ireland's Geographic Features

Area: 27,133 square miles (70,274 sq km)

Highest Elevation: Carrantuohill, 3,415 feet (1,041 m) above sea level

Lowest Elevation: North Slob, county Wexford, 10 feet (3 m) below sea level

Longest River: Shannon, 240 miles (386 km)

Largest Lake: Lough Corrib, 69 square miles (179 sq km)

Highest Waterfall: Powerscourt Waterfall, 398 feet (121 m)

Average Daily High Temperature: In Dublin, 48°F (9°C) in January, 68°F (20°C) in July

Average Daily Low Temperature: In Dublin, 39°F (4°C) in January, 56°F (13°C) in July

Average Annual Precipitation: 21 inches (53 cm) in Dublin; 48 inches (122 cm) in Cork

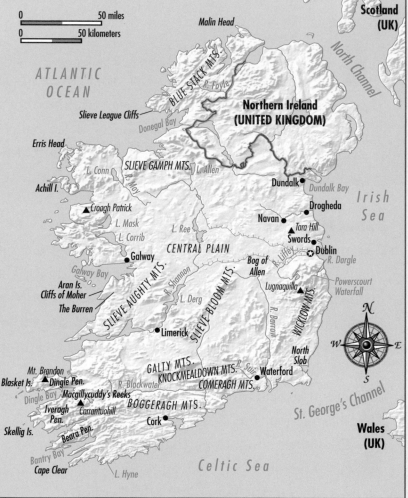

Along the coasts, most often in the west, are features called corries. The name comes from an Irish word meaning "kettle." Corries are half-circle hollows with steep sides. Each corrie was dug out by a glacier moving through a valley.

The retreating ice scraped away almost all of the soil in the northern counties of Donegal and Tyrone. The soil in that area is very thin and of little use in agriculture.

Central and Eastern Ireland

The island of Ireland is shaped something like a bowl. In the center is a flat plain, which is almost completely surrounded by mountains.

Some lakes, such as this one in the Sheeffry Hills of county Mayo, were formed when corries filled with water.

Early morning mist surrounds the ruins of an ancient monastery in the Wicklow Mountains.

The Central Plain forms a wide belt across the middle of the country. In the east, between the border with Northern Ireland and the Wicklow Mountains south of Dublin, this flat area extends all the way to the Irish Sea, which separates Ireland from Great Britain. The Wicklow Mountains are the main mountain range in the east. Lugnaquilla, the highest peak in the Wicklows, reaches 3,035 feet (925 meters). The Wicklow Mountains are home to Powerscourt Waterfall, the highest waterfall in Ireland. At this falls, the River Dargle rushes over a drop of 398 feet (121 m). Major mountain ranges south of the Central Plain include the Knockmealdown and Comeragh Mountains.

Western Ireland

The west of Ireland is wilder and more mountainous than the east. In the southwest, glaciers carved out valleys between rows of parallel mountains. These mountain ranges extend onto rugged peninsulas that jut out into the Atlantic, including the Dingle, Iveragh, and Beara Peninsulas. The valleys between them are now deep bays, such as Dingle and Bantry, which separate the peninsulas.

The peninsulas feature hiking trails that the Irish and visitors alike often follow to explore the countryside. But watch out—what the Irish call "hill walking" can be an adventure scrambling up steep and slippery mountain trails.

A road called the Ring of Kerry circles the Iveragh Peninsula, showing off county Kerry's beautiful scenery.

The Burren

Most of Ireland is green, but a section of counties Clare and Galway is an exception. This region is called the Burren, which means "great rock." It is hilly land of 50 square miles (130 square kilometers) of barren limestone, ending in cliffs that drop down into the Atlantic Ocean. The rock was wiped clean long ago by glaciers. Little grows on the rock itself, but grasses and weeds grow in the cracks. Some of these plants are found only in the Burren.

As much as five thousand years ago, people made tombs in the Burren. The tombs feature a flat slab of rock capping a group of standing rocks. These structures are called dolmens. There are hundreds of dolmens and other ancient stone structures in the Burren.

Carrantuohill, Ireland's highest peak at 3,415 feet (1,041 m) above sea level, rises in the Macgillycuddy's Reeks mountain range on the southeastern end of the Iveragh Peninsula. The 122-mile-long (196-kilometer) Beara Way trail rings the Beara Peninsula in the southwestern corner of Ireland, offering peaceful landscapes and pleasant villages.

North of these peninsulas, the mouth of the River Shannon forms a huge estuary, where ocean water mixes with freshwater. The Shannon is the longest river in Ireland.

Farther north is county Clare, which offers some of Ireland's most striking scenery. It can seem like you've reached the edge

About 40 percent of the Beara Way is on roads. The remainder cuts across the land on trails.

of the world when you are standing at the top of the Cliffs of Moher. These cliffs stretch along 5 miles (8 km) of coastline and drop a dizzying 702 feet (214 m) into the Atlantic Ocean. The dramatic Cliffs of Moher are one of Ireland's top tourist attractions. But Ireland's coastline also features many other magnificent cliffs. The Slieve League Cliffs in Donegal, in northwestern Ireland, are much higher than Moher. They feature a drop of 1,972 feet (601 m) to the sea.

At the foot of many Irish mountains are lakes. The largest lake in the Republic of Ireland is Lough Corrib in county Galway, which covers 69 square miles (178 sq km). The Galway River (also called River Corrib) connects the lake to the ocean.

Tourists peer over the edge of the Cliffs of Moher. More than eight hundred thousand people visited the cliffs in 2011.

The remains of an ancient monastery and graveyard still stand on Skellig Michael.

Islands

Ireland's largest island is Achill, which lies off the coast of county Mayo on the west. A bridge has connected it to mainland Ireland since 1887. Much of the island is covered by damp land called bog. Several villages occupy the drier places on the island.

South of Achill is Clare Island. There lie the ruins of a castle once owned by Grace O'Malley, who was known as a pirate queen. She was the chieftain of the O'Malley clan. Having learned the trade of shipping from her father, she and her followers got great delight out of harassing English ships.

Farther south, off the coast of Galway, lie the Aran Islands. The Aran Islands are barren and the weather can be harsh, so the people who live there must be hardy. Many mainlanders built second homes on Aran during the early 2000s, but they abandoned the homes when the economy suffered a severe downturn. Scattered across the islands are small stone beehive-shaped huts, called *clocháns*, built out of piled flat rocks. Christian hermits who wanted to live alone so they could focus on prayer may have used these huts long ago.

Skellig Michael is one of a pair of rocky islands that jut above the waves off the coast of the Iveragh Peninsula. Skellig Michael bears the remains of a monastery built in about the seventh century CE. The monks who lived there were isolated from other people, so they could devote their thoughts and energy to religion. Today, people can visit Skellig Michael only in good weather. Nearby Little Skellig is inhabited only by birds.

The Abandoned Islands

Many small islands lie off the coast of Ireland. Some of these islands were once populated but aren't anymore. About 175 people once lived on Great Blasket Island, off the coast of county Kerry. But gradually, the population declined. In 1953, the island's last 22 residents left Great Blasket when the government said it could no longer guarantee that the small population could always be rescued when threatened by big storms. Bad weather had sometimes isolated the people of Great Blasket from the mainland for weeks at a time. Today, visitors take a ferry to the island to explore the ruined houses and enjoy the beautiful surroundings.

Climate

Ireland is often called the Emerald Isle because its landscape is so green. It is green in part because it gets a significant amount of rain throughout the year. Most winds blow in from the Atlantic Ocean, making the western part of the country particularly damp. The west-facing mountain slopes in the west get four times as much rain as Dublin does. December and January are the wettest months. April is usually the driest.

Ireland lies at about the same latitude, or distance from the North Pole, as Newfoundland in Canada, but the climates of the two places are very different. Newfoundland has frigid temperatures and extensive snowfall, while the climate in Ireland is mild. This is mainly because of the North Atlantic Current, a continuation of the Gulf Stream. This current brings warm water from near the U.S. state of Florida northeast across the Atlantic. The warm current keeps Ireland, as well as Great Britain and other parts of Europe, warmer in winter than would normally be expected for their latitudes.

The interior of Ireland has warmer summers and colder winters than the coastal areas. The highest temperature ever recorded in Ireland was 92 degrees Fahrenheit (33 degrees Celsius) at Kilkenny, in the southeast, on June 26, 1887. The lowest recorded temperature was −2°F (−19°C) in county Sligo, in the west, on January 16, 1881. During the winter, the temperature in Ireland sometimes falls below freezing. Higher elevations often see light snow. Because the weather in Ireland can change so quickly, almost everyone dresses in layers. Sweaters are removed or added as needed.

Ireland's Largest Cities

Dublin, the capital of Ireland, is almost ten times larger than any of the republic's other cities, with a population of 1,110,627 in 2011. But the others each have their own character and play important roles in the country's culture and economy.

Cork (below), which lies on the south coast, is the nation's second-largest city, with a population of 198,582. The settlement that became Cork was founded as a monastery in about 603 CE by St. Finbarr. Today, he is the patron saint of Cork, which has become a bustling university, industrial, and port town. Cork has a new opera house, many art galleries, and a major school of music at the University College Cork. The Cork Jazz Festival each October draws visitors from all over the world.

The nation's third-largest city is Limerick, which is home to about 91,454 people. The city is located on the River Shannon. It was founded as a Viking settlement in about 812. Two of its major landmarks date

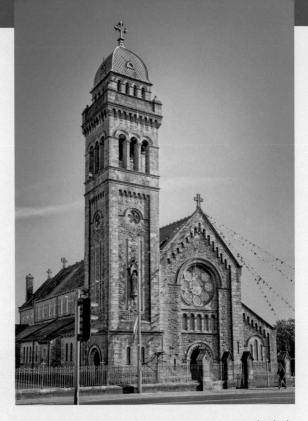

back almost a thousand years. St. Mary's Cathedral (above) was built in the 1100s and King John's Castle was built in the early 1200s. Sitting on a major river, the city grew into a center of trade. Originally, Limerick dealt mainly in agricultural products, but today it is the center of technological development.

Galway, Ireland's fourth-largest city with a population of 76,778, was founded as a fort in 1124. Today, the city is known for both its medieval buildings and its lively arts scene. Activity in the small city centers on Eyre Square. All kinds of music thrive in Galway, but the city is particularly a center of traditional Irish music. The city holds many festivals and other cultural events that draw visitors from all over the world. The Galway Arts Festival has been held each July since 1978. Galway is also a central area for the Irish language—about 10 percent of its residents speak Irish.

CHAPTER 3

Natural Ireland

IRELAND IS A VERY GREEN PLACE, BUT IT HAS A SMALLER variety of plant life than is found elsewhere in Europe. When rising seas cut Ireland off from the mainland, it became more difficult for the seeds of varied plants to be brought there. It also became more difficult for animals to migrate there. No snake species are native to Ireland. Legend has it that this is because St. Patrick drove all the snakes off the island. The actual reason is that during the last ice age, the land was too cold for snakes and other reptiles to survive there. Then, when the glaciers melted and Ireland became an island, snakes had no easy way of migrating from continental Europe.

Opposite: **Heather blooms on Roundstone Bog in county Galway.**

From Forests to Bogs

After the last ice age ended, dense forests grew rapidly in Ireland. These forests were filled with hardwood trees such as oak. As people began farming in Ireland thousands of years ago, the trees were cut down, especially on hillsides. Frequent rain striking the slopes washed the nutrients out of the soil and turned it slightly acidic. In place of forests, wet, soft land called bogs developed.

The Irish have planted many trees in recent years, and today about 10 percent of the country is now planted in what will become forests. The trees being planted are Sitka spruce rather than the hardwoods that once grew on the island.

Bogs now cover about one-sixth of the land in Ireland. They form in places where the water cannot drain away. Over time, the water loses its oxygen, and most plants can no longer grow there. Only small, soft plants called mosses can survive in such water. The lack of oxygen in the water also

Torc Waterfall rushes through the woods in county Kerry, in the west of Ireland.

slows down the rotting of the plants after they die, because rotting is a chemical process that requires oxygen. So in bogs, as each generation of plants dies, the dead plants accumulate, gradually forming a deeper and deeper layer. The plant matter slowly turns into a material called peat.

Ireland has two kinds of bogs. Blanket bogs look almost like a flat stretch of grass. They are mostly in the west, where there is plenty of rain, and in the mountains. Raised bogs develop mostly on low-lying land that once was a lake or a marsh. Such bogs gradually develop a domed, or raised, shape. The center of Ireland is a huge, raised bog called the Bog of Allen. At its center is Croghan Hill, an ancient volcano.

Frequently, woody plants called heath or heather grow in bogs, using the moss as footing. But they don't grow tall, so the landscape still looks fairly barren. The heath may have a purplish tinge from the tiny flowers on the heather plants. Some insect-eating plants, such as sundew and butterwort, live in bogs. They can't get nourishment from the bog, so they trap insects on sticky leaves and digest them as food.

A Farm in the Bog

More than five thousand years ago, some Stone Age inhabitants of what is now county Mayo had a farm that included houses, stone walls, and even tombs. Over many years, a blanket bog covered the land, gradually becoming deeper and deeper. In the 1930s, a teacher cutting peat realized that there were stones deep in the peat that could not have settled there naturally. His son, Seamus Caulfield, became an archaeologist, a person who studies the remnants of ancient people. In the 1970s, Caulfield realized that the bog was covering an ancient farm. The prehistoric inhabitants had raised cattle and cleared forests. Now called Céide Fields, it is the largest Stone Age site and oldest known field system in the world.

Mammals

Because Ireland was cut off from the rest of Europe, it has relatively few mammal species. Fifty-five types of mammals are considered native to Ireland, but only twenty-six of those are land species. Ireland's ocean waters, especially in the south

Seals emerge from the water near the Blasket Islands. The Blaskets are a major breeding ground for gray seals.

and west, attract dolphins. Bottlenose dolphins frequently swim into the Shannon estuary. A dolphin called Fungie has entranced visitors in Dingle Harbor for several decades. Killer whales, also known as orcas, can often be seen from shore.

Irish hares can reach speeds of up to 30 miles per hour (50 kph).

The Wolfhound

Ireland's official dog is the Irish wolfhound, whose ancestors probably came to the island with humans thousands of years ago. It is the tallest of all dog breeds, reaching an average of about 34 inches (86 centimeters) at the neck. When standing on its hind feet, the Irish wolfhound is taller than most men. Irish wolfhounds can weigh as much as 180 pounds (82 kilograms). They were first bred for their speed and skill at running down wolves. This is no longer a useful skill in Ireland, because there have not been any wolves in Ireland since about 1786.

Seals frequently come ashore, especially around Cork Harbor. They almost became extinct back in the 1950s and 1960s, but laws were passed to protect them, and their numbers have increased. Most of the animals are Atlantic gray seals or the smaller common or harbor seals.

Most of the nation's mammals are small land mammals. Many members of the weasel family, including otters and stoats, live there. The mink was introduced. The gray squirrel was also introduced, in about 1911. The red squirrel is native

Unlike most deer, fallow deer keep their spots even as adults.

The largest deer species that ever existed was the Irish elk. This species is extinct, but its remains have been found in peat bogs in Ireland. The Irish elk lived before the last ice age. It probably died off because it couldn't withstand the increasing cold. Some of the Irish elk fossils that have been uncovered have antlers 12 feet (4 m) across.

to Ireland but is becoming rare. A species of hare related to the Arctic hare lives in Ireland. Arctic hares turn white in the winter, but Irish hares do not. In Ireland, hares are welcome food for birds of prey. Ireland is also home to European rabbits and prickly little hedgehogs. Many foxes also live in Ireland.

Red deer, also called stag deer, live throughout Ireland. They are Ireland's official animal. Ireland's English rulers introduced the fallow deer into Ireland nine hundred years ago. The sika deer was introduced by an owner of a large estate about 150 years ago. Some of the deer escaped and formed herds in the wild.

Birds

About 250 species of birds live in Ireland or visit frequently. Wrens, robins, and blackbirds are common. Many kinds of warblers, finches, and buntings are seen throughout the country. Ireland has large populations of seabirds, such as whooper swans, white-fronted and barnacle geese, and terns. Puffins nest in colonies along the coasts. Little Skellig Island holds the world's second-largest colony of breeding northern gannets.

Common birds of prey include peregrines, merlins, harriers, and choughs (which are related to crows). But many

A basking shark feeds in the Irish Sea. Basking sharks are the second-largest fish living today, trailing only whale sharks.

kinds of birds of prey that once lived in Ireland have been hunted out of existence. The last golden eagle in Ireland was seen in 1912. Irish wildlife experts introduced young golden eagles into Glenveagh National Park in 2005. One pair has produced several chicks. They feed off the hares in the park.

Red kites have also disappeared. Once in a while one appears, probably blown in from Wales, across the Irish Sea. They are being reintroduced throughout the country, especially in the Dublin area. More than 120 birds have been released. The public has been warned not to use rat poison, because the kites eat rats and can die from the poison.

Fish and Reptiles

Ireland's rivers and lakes abound with fish, about forty species in all. Common fish found in Ireland include bream, pike, and trout. Fish found in Ireland's ocean waters include cod, mackerel, eels, and sharks.

National Parks

Ireland has six national parks. Many of them feature beautiful houses or historic sites in addition to stunning scenery. Most also have untouched bog land.

Wicklow Mountains National Park is south of Dublin. It features heath and bog landscape. Glendalough Valley, which runs through the park, includes the ruins of the ancient monastery of St. Kevin.

Killarney National Park lies in the southwest, in county Kerry. It includes the MacGillycuddy's Reeks, Ireland's highest mountains. A beautiful nineteenth-century mansion called Muckross House (below) is located in the park.

The Burren, in county Clare, is Ireland's smallest national park. Of Ireland's thirty-three species of butterfly, most of them are found in the Burren. One species, called the Burren green, lives only in the Burren.

Connemara National Park (above), in county Galway, contains the Twelve Bens range, which includes mountains such as Benbaun, Bencullagh, and Benbrack. (*Ben* means "mountain peak.")

North of Connemara is Ballycroy National Park in county Mayo, the nation's newest national park. Most of it is uninhabited and covered by a vast blanket bog, one of the last big bogs of Europe.

Glenveagh National Park lies in county Donegal, in the northwest. It features rugged mountains, pristine lakes, a castle, and many gardens. Ireland's largest herd of red deer roams the land.

Sea turtles also swim in the waters off Ireland's west coast. These large reptiles occasionally come ashore. The only land reptile native to Ireland is the viviparous lizard. Unlike most reptiles, this lizard gives birth to live young rather than laying eggs. It is often found in the Wicklow Mountains.

CHAPTER 4

The Long Road to Independence

BEFORE THE LAST ICE AGE, HUMANS MAY HAVE lived in the region that is now Ireland, but there is no record of it. As the ice retreated, people walked north from Europe across a land bridge to Great Britain and then to Ireland. As the ice continued to melt, the sea rose and filled the areas between the continent and Great Britain and Ireland. The land bridge disappeared beneath the waves.

Opposite: **Poulnabrone Dolmen is a tomb that was built in the Burren at least five thousand years ago. More than twenty people are buried under the massive monument.**

Ancient Ireland

The early people who settled in Ireland probably began planting fields for crops by 5000 BCE. Archaeologists have found pottery, stone tools, and the outlines of small houses. Soon, the ancient people of Ireland also began to build stone monuments that still stand today. One found at Newgrange, north of Dublin, is older than the pyramids of ancient Egypt. On the winter solstice, December 21, the shortest day of the year, the rising sun lights up passages deep within the burial chambers.

People called Celts began arriving from the continent during the seventh century BCE. In the following centuries, more waves of Celts arrived. The Celtic people were primarily farmers and cattle ranchers.

Land Bridge 6,000 Years Ago

Ancient land
Present land
Present-day border

The Arrival of Christianity

It is often said that St. Patrick (ca. 387–461?) brought Christianity to Ireland, but stories about Jesus Christ and the religion he founded had already begun to circulate on the island a hundred years or more before Patrick arrived there. The Romans, who controlled Britain at that time, probably introduced these stories. Palladius, a bishop in Britain, visited Ireland in about 431 but did not do much to convert people to Christianity.

Patrick, who was probably born in Scotland, had been brought to Ireland as a slave as a young man. After several years, he escaped and made his way to the continent, where he became a priest. He returned to Ireland in 432 as a bishop. He found fertile ground for his beliefs and was determined to convert the entire island. Before his death, he had built more than 350 small churches around the island.

The Irish took to Christianity quickly. They founded many monasteries, which attracted scholars from Europe. Irish monks created the first written Irish literature. They used the Roman alphabet introduced by St. Patrick to record Irish tales, sermons, and even medical advice. Ireland became an important center of Christian arts and culture.

The monks added elaborate illustrations to the manuscripts they made, an art called illumination. One of the most beautiful illuminated manuscripts is the Book of Kells, which was created around the year 800. It was held for hundreds of years at the Abbey of Kells, in county Meath. Today, the Book of Kells is at the Trinity College Library in Dublin.

The Book of Kells is famed for its swirling, complex decoration. Here, an abbreviation in Greek for the word *Christ* includes angels, insects, and animals amid the decorative patterns.

The Vikings Arrive

In about 795, Vikings from Norway reached Ireland. They started raiding communities and churches, especially on the western islands. Irish people were sometimes kidnapped and sold as slaves. Later, the Vikings began to settle in Ireland. In 841, Vikings seized control of a religious settlement on the east coast. They turned that settlement into the Kingdom of Dublin. Viking settlements at Limerick, Waterford, Cork, and Wexford became Ireland's largest cities.

The Norse attacked the monastery of Clonmacnoise at least seven times between 800 and 1200.

The Norse settlers gradually began to live like the Irish around them. The two populations eventually merged. However, the Norse retained control of Dublin until 980, when an Irish king later called Malachy the Great defeated the Norse at the Battle of Tara. High King Brian Boru later took control of Ireland from Malachy.

English Invasions

The Vikings were not the only Norse people to come to Ireland. The Normans were originally Norsemen who had settled in what became France. The Normans took control of England in

ATLANTIC OCEAN

Tara 980

Confey 917

Dublin

Clontarf 1014

Luimnech 968

Sulcoit 968

Limerick

Wexford

Waterford

Cork

Irish Sea

Viking Ireland

Area settled by Vikings

• Viking settlement

✕ Major battle

The High Kings

Ireland was divided into many small kingdoms. At various times, one king would become particularly powerful and declare himself a high king. Some high kings ruled from the Hill of Tara, west of Dublin. This was especially true during the O'Neill dynasty. But how much power the high kings had is not known.

The most famous high king was Brian Boru (left). He conquered the O'Neill dynasty and founded a new dynasty, the O'Briens. King Brian Boru defeated the Norse at Dublin in 1014 in the Battle of Clontarf, ending Norse power in Ireland.

English leader Strongbow and his troops quickly captured Waterford and Dublin.

1066. In 1155, Pope Adrian IV, the leader of the Roman Catholic Church, encouraged King Henry II of England to invade Ireland. He did this because he thought the Irish church was too independent and needed to be brought more firmly under the control of Rome. Thus began seven centuries of revolt, repression, and rebellion.

In 1169, Ireland was invaded by the army of an English leader nicknamed Strongbow. Strongbow earned his name from his amazing skill with a bow and arrow. His true name was Richard de Clare, Earl of Pembroke. He was invited into Ireland by an angry king named Dermot MacMurrough. High King Rory O'Connor had removed Dermot from his throne after Dermot had sworn an oath of allegiance to Henry II. With Strongbow's help, Dermot got his kingship back, but then Henry sent troops into Ireland and proclaimed himself Lord of Ireland.

The Anglo-Normans (Normans from England) occupied Ireland. Many became landholders who owned large estates and lived off the rents paid by Irish tenants.

In 1297, a parliament was created for Ireland. Only the Anglo-Irish, however, were represented in the parliament. The native Irish, often referred to as Gaelic Irish, had no representation.

A meeting of the ancient Irish Parliament. The main purpose of the parliament was to approve taxes.

Hugh O'Neill, the earl of Tyrone, spent many years fighting English rule, but in 1607 he and his family left Ireland in the Flight of the Earls.

Oppression and Rebellion

In the 1500s, new battles arose in Ireland after England broke away from the Roman Catholic Church. English king Henry VIII declared himself the head of the Church of England, also known as the Anglican Church. England was now a Protestant nation and sought to impose Protestantism on Ireland. But the Gaelic Irish would not stand for it. Nor would many of the Anglo-Irish landholders. Time and again, English soldiers fought the Irish nobles, hoping to make them give up the Catholic Church.

Instead, in 1607, several leading nobles in the northern part of the country fled to Europe, abandoning Ireland forever. This event came to be called the Flight of the Earls.

The English continued to fight to gain complete control of the Irish. In 1641, there was a major Irish rebellion. It failed, and angered the English even more. English leader Oliver Cromwell disliked the Irish and hated Catholicism. He invaded Ireland in 1649. Tens of thousands of Irish people, civilians as well as soldiers, died as Cromwell further tightened England's grip on Ireland.

The Protestant Ascendancy

During the wars to conquer Ireland, the Protestant English had frequently confiscated land from Catholics. By 1703, Catholics owned less than 15 percent of the land in Ireland, though they made up the vast majority of the population.

About one-tenth of the population belonged to the Anglican Church. They became the ruling class of Ireland, known

Many political leaders in England and Ireland mistrusted the Catholic Church. This cartoon shows the church as the Big Bad Wolf about to gobble up Little Red Riding Hood, who represents Ireland.

as the Protestant Ascendancy. In the 1600s and 1700s, many laws were passed taking away rights from Catholics as well as from Protestants who did not belong to the Anglican Church. Catholics and non-Anglican Protestants could not hold public office. Catholics could not own firearms, serve in the military, or be teachers. Beginning in 1728, Catholics were not allowed to vote. Catholics could not marry Protestants, and Protestants could not convert to Catholicism. These and many similar laws were called the Penal Laws. They were meant to force Catholics and members of minority Protestant groups to accept the Anglican Church.

But the people of Ireland did not give up their faiths. Catholics continued to worship in their own way, often in secret, and they rebelled when they could.

Members of the Protestant Ascendancy soon grew to dislike how the British treated Ireland. They were frustrated that the British Parliament made laws for Ireland and got in the way of its economic growth. They, too, would soon be rebelling.

Rebellion and Union

In 1798, some of the Protestant Ascendancy joined forces with Catholic leaders to gain greater self-government for Ireland. A Protestant named Wolfe Tone tried to get France to help the Irish in their rebellion. The British government encouraged Irish Protestants to break away from the Catholics. During this struggle, one rebellion would be suppressed, and another would break out. Wolfe Tone and the French troops eventually arrived, but the British defeated them. Tone, sentenced to be hanged, committed suicide before he could be executed. The 1798 Rising (another word for rebellion) was probably the most violent in Irish history. It is estimated that more than twenty thousand people died in the fighting.

In response to the rebellion, Britain tightened its control on Ireland. The 1801 Act of Union made Ireland part of the United Kingdom of Great Britain and Ireland. The Irish Parliament was dissolved, and Irish representatives were sent to Parliament in London.

Many Irish people disliked that Ireland was now fully joined with the United Kingdom. They continued to fight for their rights. Catholics began

Wolfe Tone helped found the Society of United Irishmen. This organization, made up primarily of Protestants such as Tone, worked to gain Catholic rights in Ireland.

demanding more freedom. A lawyer named Daniel O'Connell led the effort to help Catholics gain political rights. In 1828, he was elected to the British Parliament from county Clare, but as a Catholic, he could not take his seat. Rather than risk the rising fury of the Catholic population, in 1829, the British changed the law. Catholics were finally allowed in Parliament, and O'Connell took his seat.

This cartoon shows British prime minister William Pitt (far right) resigning from office when King George III refused to allow Irish Catholics to vote as part of the 1801 Act of Union.

Daniel O'Connell was nicknamed the Liberator. He organized a series of huge meetings across Ireland at which Catholics pressured Britain for the right to vote and hold public office.

The Great Famine

Ireland at this time was primarily rural. Most of the farmers worked land they rented from wealthy landlords. All the corn, barley, dairy products, and meat they raised went to the landlords, who sold it in England. The potato was the main food of the impoverished Irish farmers who grew these products.

The potato had originated in South America. It was not brought to Ireland until the latter half of the sixteenth century. Gradually, it replaced the oats and barley the poor people had previously eaten.

But in the mid-1840s, a fungus infested the potato crop in Ireland. The plants turned black and inedible. The poor people of Ireland had nothing to eat. They began to starve,

Hungry Irish farmers huddle around a fire. During the Great Famine, Ireland's population dropped by about one-quarter because so many people died of starvation or left the country.

but the landlords continued to send all the other food products to England. It is estimated that at least one million Irish people died during the Great Famine, which lasted from 1845 to 1849. Another one million people left Ireland forever. Half of them went to the United States. The population of Ireland has never again been as large as it was before the famine.

The Home Rule Movement

The Irish Republican Brotherhood was founded in 1858. Its members planned for an armed rebellion. They wanted Ireland to become a republic, completely independent from Britain. As this movement grew in Ireland, the British recognized the need for change. In 1870, the Irish Land Act was put into effect, which helped protect tenants from being evicted from their homes.

That same year, the Home Rule movement began to grow in Ireland. The idea of Home Rule was that the Irish would govern themselves but remain part of the United Kingdom. The Home Rule movement managed to force Parliament to at least discuss the possibility of Home Rule for the Irish.

Home Rule was voted on in Parliament twice, but it was defeated both times. "Home Rule is Rome rule," some people who opposed it said, meaning that the Catholic Church would rule Ireland if Home Rule was established. The third time Parliament

Officials evict a tenant farmer from his home for not paying the rent. Hundreds of thousands of Irish people were evicted between 1849 and 1880.

Parnell and Land Reform

An important leader in the Home Rule movement was Charles Stewart Parnell. He was a Protestant landowner who became the leader of the Home Rule Party and served in the British Parliament. Parnell also headed the Irish National Land League, which fought to prevent the eviction of farmers from their land and to reduce the rents the farmers had to pay. To bring attention to the problem, Parnell slowed down the work of Parliament by giving long speeches. The British prime minister was eventually forced to propose a law establishing fair rents and allowing some farmers to buy the land they farmed.

voted on Home Rule, in 1912, it finally passed, but the law never went into effect because the fighting that became World War I soon began, involving all of Europe in other concerns.

The Critical Years

Many people who wanted to see Ireland become independent fought in the British army during World War I. But some who remained at home continued to organize the fight against the British. The Irish Republican Brotherhood made plans to take over the General Post Office in Dublin on Easter Monday, April 24, 1916, and proclaim that Ireland was a republic, no longer under the rule of the British monarchy. The Easter Rising, as it is known, didn't work. Within five days, the fighting had damaged large parts of Dublin. Killed were 157 British soldiers, 82 rebels, and more than 200 civilians. Many members of the public did not support the rebels. They felt that with British and Irish forces dying in Europe, the timing was wrong.

Last Port of Call

The town of Cobh (Irish for "cove"), formerly called Queenstown, is located on an island in a great natural harbor near Cork. Because of its location, Queenstown was for many years the last port of call for the large ocean liners heading to America. It was the last glimpse of home for most immigrants leaving Ireland (left). On April 12, 1912, Queenstown was the last port for the brand-new luxury liner the RMS *Titanic*, before it made its first trip across the Atlantic Ocean. Two days later, the passenger liner struck an iceberg in the North Atlantic. Before help could arrive, the great ship sank. More than 1,500 people died.

But when the British executed fifteen of the leaders of the rebellion, Irish public opinion turned in favor of Irish independence. In the 1918 election, the Irish people elected seventy-three members of the political party Sinn Féin (Irish for "We Ourselves") to the British Parliament. The group was led by Éamon de Valera. Instead of taking their seats in the British Parliament, they formed the first Dáil (pronounced DOYL), or Irish Parliament.

Meanwhile, the Irish Republican Army, or IRA, was fighting against British forces in Ireland. They fought a guerrilla war, attacking soldiers or supplies to get weapons and then disappearing back into the general population. This conflict is called the Anglo-Irish War, or the Irish War of Independence.

A member of Sinn Féin named Michael Collins was the director of intelligence for the Irish Republican Army. In this role, he coordinated attacks on the British. On November 21,

1920, Collins and his group gunned down fourteen British undercover agents. Later that day, the angry police fired into the crowd at a Gaelic football match, killing fourteen civilians. Within months, more than 4,500 Irish fighters had been imprisoned. Sinn Féin decided to start negotiating peace.

Free State soldiers take aim at forces opposing the Anglo-Irish Treaty during the Irish Civil War.

An End to British Rule

A truce was called in 1921. In the Anglo-Irish Treaty of 1921, the British and the Irish worked out a system that divided

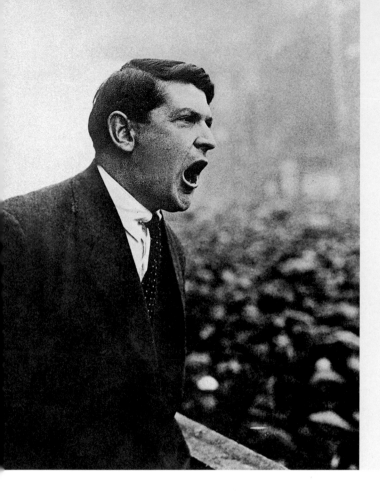

Michael Collins, Irish Hero

Michael Collins, born in county Cork, was a clerk in London, England, when he joined the Irish Republican Brotherhood and began working for Irish independence. He returned to Dublin to fight in the Easter Rising of 1916. He took its failures to heart. He knew that the Irish fighters could not confront the British head-on. He joined Sinn Féin, and was elected to Parliament in 1918. Like the other Sinn Féin members of Parliament, Collins did not take his seat. Instead, together they set up the first Irish Parliament. Since the president, Éamon de Valera, and many of the other newly elected members of Parliament were in jail, Collins played a large role in the Irish Parliament.

Collins was an important figure in the negotiation of the Anglo-Irish Treaty. He disliked that the Irish would have to swear an oath of allegiance to the British crown, but he thought it was the best treaty that could be negotiated at the time. On August 22, 1922, Collins was shot and killed by an Irish fighter opposed to the treaty.

Ireland, creating two separate governments. The six counties in the northeast that had large Protestant populations became known as Northern Ireland. It remained part of Great Britain. The remainder of the island became a separate nation called the Irish Free State.

Under the treaty, the Irish were self-ruling, but they still had to swear an oath of allegiance to the British crown. Many Irish people were angry about this and opposed the treaty. They wanted nothing less than a republic. The IRA split over the treaty, and a civil war began. The fighting continued until 1923.

Éamon de Valera was a leader in the Irish War of Independence. He remained a major force in Irish politics until the 1970s.

In the 1930s, the seeds of what would become World War II were growing across Europe. Ireland declared itself neutral. The British needed Irish ports for their military ships. They even offered to reunite the two parts of Ireland if the Free State would give up its neutrality. The Irish refused.

At this time, the king of the United Kingdom was still the official head of state of Ireland. Although that had little effect on Irish people, many of them talked about separating completely from Great Britain. Nothing was done, though, until 1948, when Ireland became a republic. This ended Ireland's relationship with the British monarchy. After eight hundred years, the Irish were no longer British subjects.

The Celtic Tiger

After Ireland became independent, it continued to struggle economically. Talented people left to find their fortunes elsewhere. Finally, in the 1970s, the Irish government realized that great changes were needed if Ireland was going to compete with other nations. It started by joining the European Economic Community (EEC), which later became the European Union (EU).

Double-decker buses run up and down O'Connell Street, a grand road through the heart of Dublin, in the 1960s. At the time, Dublin had about seven hundred thousand residents.

The Troubles

After Ireland was divided, Catholics in Northern Ireland were often discriminated against. A civil rights movement began in the 1960s. By the early 1970s, some Catholics had decided that the best solution would be for Northern Ireland to join the Republic of Ireland. Most of the Protestants in Northern Ireland wanted to remain part of the United Kingdom. Violence flared, beginning in the 1960s, and continued on and off for decades. This period is known as the Troubles.

Most of the violence was in Northern Ireland, but it sometimes spilled over into the republic. For example, on May 17, 1974, three car bombs exploded in Dublin (left), killing twenty-six people. In all, about 3,500 people died during the conflict.

The Troubles finally came to an end with the Good Friday Agreement of 1998. Part of the agreement said that Northern Ireland would be part of Britain until the majority of the citizens decided they wanted to join the republic. In 1998, the Nobel Peace Prize went jointly to two Northern Irish men. John Hume (above, right), a Catholic, and David Trimble (above, left), a Protestant, received the prize for their roles in negotiating the Good Friday Agreement.

After Ireland joined the EEC in 1973, it received a great deal of money to help it develop its economy. EEC funds built roads, improved tourist sites, and gave funds to farmers. Joining the EEC also opened up new markets for goods throughout Europe. Ireland began to prosper. Some Irish people who had immigrated returned home.

Ireland was also becoming more attractive to corporations. Ireland had a population of English-speaking, well-educated workers. Then, in the late 1990s, when the Dáil lowered the tax rate paid by corporations, major companies from the United States and elsewhere came to Ireland. Microsoft, Dell, Intel, Johnson & Johnson, Pfizer, and other companies moved some of their facilities to Ireland. Suddenly, good, well-paying jobs were easy to come by in Ireland. This period, from 1995 to 2008, is called the Celtic Tiger.

The American company Intel is the world's largest maker of computer chips. The town of Leixlip, just west of Dublin, is home to Intel's largest manufacturing plant outside the United States.

Boom and Bust

The sudden increase in money available to the Irish meant that average people could buy houses for themselves, most of them for the first time. Prices rose quickly. Housing prices rose by more than 500 percent in twelve years. People who worked in Dublin but could not afford to live there were buying houses as much as 75 miles (120 km) away, a very long commute on Ireland's twisty roads. Banks lent money to almost anyone who wanted to buy or build a house, whether they could afford it or not.

In 2008, the global economy went into a severe economic downturn. The government used public money to guarantee

Ireland experienced a building boom during the Celtic Tiger years. The Convention Centre Dublin was completed in 2010.

loans made by the nation's six largest banks. But the government did not have enough money to take on all these loans. Ireland was forced to borrow billions of dollars from the European Union. This money is called a bailout. Most of the bailout went to keeping the banks from collapsing. There was little money left to help the people who could no longer afford to pay the loans on their houses.

Many housing estates or developments that had been started were never finished. These "ghost estates" stand as symbols of the excess of those years.

As the economy slowed, many people lost their jobs. Once again, thousands of young people decided to leave Ireland for greater opportunity elsewhere. The Irish continue to work to get their country back on its feet. They know that it will take time to achieve the good life again.

Houses stand empty and incomplete in a "ghost estate" in North Dublin. The nation has nearly three thousand unfinished housing developments.

CHAPTER 5

Governing the Republic

IRELAND'S GOVERNMENT FUNCTIONS ACCORDING TO its constitution, which was written in 1937. It has been amended several times since then. To vote, a person must be eighteen years old and have lived in Ireland for at least five years. The British gave some Irish men the right to vote in 1884. Women over thirty were allowed to vote beginning in 1918. Since 1922, anyone over the age of twenty-one has been allowed to vote.

Opposite: **The Irish Parliament meets in Leinster House. Built in the 1740s, it was originally a palace for the duke of Leinster.**

The Legislature

Ireland had its own parliament even before England did. The first Irish Parliament was founded in 1297 and lasted until the end of 1800, when Ireland became part of the United Kingdom. Today, the Irish legislature, or Oireachtas (pronounced air-UHK-tuhss), consists of two houses. The lower and more powerful house is the Dáil Éireann (DOYL AIR-uhn). It has between 153 and 160 members who are elected for five-year terms. Elections may be held sooner if the members of the Dáil no longer support the prime minister.

The upper house is the Seanad Éireann (SHAN-uhd AIR-uhn), or senate. It has sixty members. Some of these senators are

Ireland had female presidents from 1990 to 2011, but it has had far fewer female legislators than other countries in western Europe have had. In 2012, only 15 percent of the members of the Dáil and 30 percent of the members of the Seanad were women. In 2012, a law was passed requiring all political parties to have at least 30 percent female candidates. After seven years, that number will rise to 40 percent.

appointed by the prime minister. Others are elected by graduates of certain universities or groups with specific areas of expertise, such as the Agricultural Panel and the Cultural and Educational Panel. The Seanad has little power in the Irish government. It can slow down laws from being enacted, but it cannot veto them, and the Dáil can override any decision that the Seanad makes. Many Irish people have called for the Seanad to be abolished. They say that it has no government function.

Leaders of the Dáil Éireann and Seanad Éireann meet with Chinese officials in 2012.

National Government of Ireland

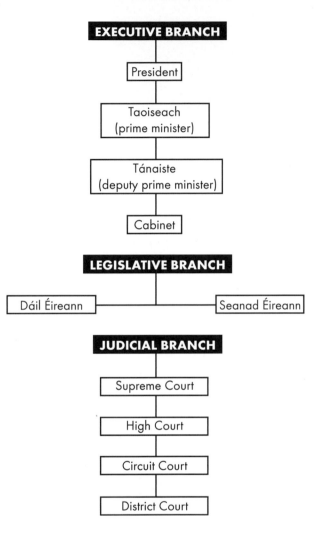

EXECUTIVE BRANCH

President

Taoiseach
(prime minister)

Tánaiste
(deputy prime minister)

Cabinet

LEGISLATIVE BRANCH

Dáil Éireann — Seanad Éireann

JUDICIAL BRANCH

Supreme Court

High Court

Circuit Court

District Court

Head of State and Government

The head of state in Ireland is the president. He or she is elected directly by the people for a seven-year term and may be elected a second time. The president must consult the Council of State when making decisions. Most of the members of the council

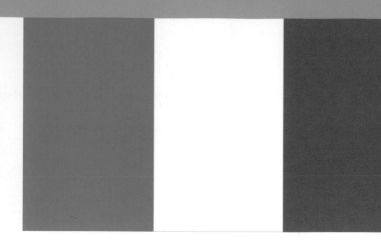

are former high officials in the government. The president can name up to seven additional members to the council.

The first female president of Ireland was Mary Robinson, who served from 1990 to 1997. She held a law degree from Harvard University in the United States and had been a senator for twenty years. After Robinson, Mary McAleese served as president from 1997 to 2011. McAleese was the first president

Irish president Mary Robinson talks with U.S. president Bill Clinton in 1995. She left office in 1997 to become the United Nations Commissioner for Human Rights.

National Anthem

Ireland's national anthem is the chorus of "The Soldiers' Song," which was written in 1907 by Peadar Kearney and Patrick Heeney. Rebels sang this song during the Easter Rising, and it was adopted as Ireland's national anthem in 1926. The anthem, called "Amhrán na bhFiann" in Irish, is always sung in Irish rather than English. Even in the English version, there are two words sung in Irish: *bearna baoil*. They mean the "gap of danger," or the space between two opposing armies.

Irish lyrics

Sinne Fianna Fáil
Atá faoi gheall ag Éirinn
Buíon dár slua
Thar toinn do ráinig chughainn
Faoi mhóid bheith saor
Sean-tír ár sinsear feasta
Ní fhágfar faoin tiorán ná faoin tráill
Anocht a théam sa bhearna baoil
Le gean ar Ghaeil chun báis nó saoil
Le gunna scréach faoi lámhach na bpiléar
Seo libh canaig Amhrán na bhFiann

English lyrics

Soldiers are we,
whose lives are pledged to Ireland,
Some have come
from a land beyond the wave,
Sworn to be free,
no more our ancient Ireland,
Shall shelter the despot or the slave.
Tonight we man the *bearna baoil*,
In Erin's cause, come woe or weal,
'Mid cannon's roar and rifle's peal,
We'll chant a soldier's song.

Enda Kenny became a member of the Dáil Éireann in 1975 and taoiseach in 2011.

of the republic to have been born in Northern Ireland. The current president, Michael D. Higgins, was inaugurated in 2011. He is a longtime member of the Labor Party.

The head of government in Ireland is the prime minister, called the *taoiseach* (TEE-shock). He or she is chosen by the political party with the most members in the Dáil and is then officially appointed by the president. The taoiseach appoints the members of the cabinet. These include the minister of finance, the minister of health, and the minister of education and skills. Most of the ministers are members of the Dáil. The taoiseach's deputy is called the *tánaiste* (TAW-nuhsh-tyuh), which means "deputy king."

The Judicial System

The highest court in Ireland is the Supreme Court, which includes a chief justice and seven other judges. The Supreme Court reviews decisions made in lower courts and interprets the constitution.

Below the Supreme Court is the High Court, which also has the power to interpret the constitution. In addition, a division of the High Court called the Central Criminal Court handles the most serious criminal cases, such as murder trials. Most trials in Ireland are held in the Circuit Court. Less serious offenses that do not require a jury are handled in the District Court. All judges are appointed by the president and serve until they retire.

Political Parties

For most of the time since Ireland became independent, its most powerful political party was Fianna Fáil (FEE-uhn-uh FOYL), which means "Soldiers of Destiny." The party was founded by Éamon de Valera in 1926. The party received much of the credit for the economic boom of the 1990s and early 2000s. But it also received the blame when the Irish economy stumbled. In 2011, Fianna Fáil lost to Fine Gael (FIN-nuh GAYL), which means "Tribe of the Irish." In 2011, Fine Gael leader Enda Kenny was elected taoiseach.

Military and Police

Ireland has only a small military force, but Irish citizens can join the armed forces of other countries, such as the United Kingdom and the United States. Irish Defense

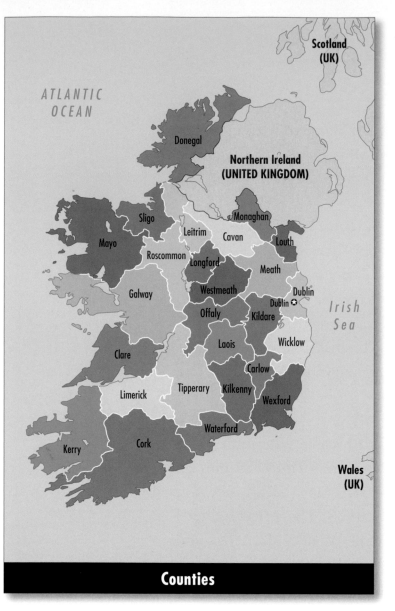

Forces have provided troops to United Nations peacekeeping operations. The defense forces include an army, navy, air corps, and reserve force.

The national police force is the Garda Síochána (GAR-duh shee-oh-CAH-nuh), usually referred to as the Gardaí, which means "guardians." An individual police officer is called a garda.

Local Government

Twenty-six counties make up the Republic of Ireland. The largest by area is Cork, in the southwest, and the smallest is Louth, in the northeast. By population, the largest is Dublin, in the east, and the smallest is Leitrim, in the west. In addition to the twenty-six counties, there are eight cities that are treated as counties.

Starting in 2014, there will be changes to local government. Some cities, such as Limerick and Waterford, are going to combine the governments of the city and county. Other counties will merge.

Dublin: The Capital City

Dublin has been the largest city in Ireland for hundreds of years. Today, it has a population of about 1.1 million people. It is located on the River Liffey on the eastern coast. The name Dublin, or Dubhlinn in Irish, means "black pool." It was founded by the Vikings at a lake (the black pool) along a tributary of the Liffey called the River Poddle.

The Liffey divides the city into north and south sections. North of the river is the business district, centered on O'Connell Street. It is named for nineteenth-century hero Daniel O'Connell, whose statue is located at one end. Also on the street is a new sculpture titled *Monument of Light*, but commonly called Spire of Dublin. Installed in 2003, it is an elegant conical pillar 398 feet (121 m) high.

Away from the downtown area is Phoenix Park, which is surrounded by a wall. It is the largest enclosed park in Europe. The official residence of Ireland's president is located in Phoenix Park. It is a white house built in the 1700s. The American ambassador's house, called Deerfield, is nearby in the park.

South of the river is Dublin Castle, built in 1204 by King John of England. It was the seat of English power in Ireland until independence. Nearby is the Roman Catholic St. Patrick's Cathedral, completed in 1191. Christ Church Cathedral, started in 1172, is the city's Protestant cathedral.

In the eighteenth century, Dublin was prosperous. Many lovely houses and other buildings were constructed in this period. Southeastern Dublin, in particular, has many buildings from this era. Grafton Street is a lively shopping street. Trinity College, where the Book of Kells is housed, is also in the southeast section.

The Royal and the Grand Canals were built in the early nineteenth century to connect Dublin with the west of Ireland. Though these canals are no longer used for barge traffic, the Royal Canal has been restored and was reopened in 2010 to recreational boats. An electric rail system called Dublin Area Rapid Transit (DART) connects the different parts of Dublin and carries people south into Wicklow.

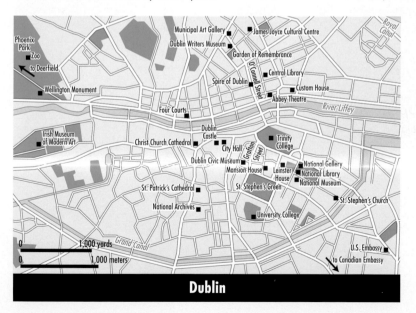

Dublin

CHAPTER 6

Making a Living

F OR MOST OF THE TWENTIETH CENTURY, IRELAND WAS one of the poorest countries in western Europe. With few jobs available in their home country, many Irish people chose to emigrate to other countries. Ireland turned its economy around in the late twentieth century and became one of the most prosperous nations in Europe. But the Celtic Tiger boom years did not last. As the world economy entered a downturn in 2008, many Irish people lost their jobs. In 2013, the unemployment rate in Ireland was still 14.6 percent.

Today, all sectors of the economy are important in Ireland. Many people work in agriculture, manufacturing, and services.

Agriculture

Almost 8 percent of the Irish people work in agriculture or fishing. Another 35 percent work in processing food. Most of what Ireland produces is exported. About 64 percent of the land in

Opposite: **Farmers feed their sheep in county Cork, in southern Ireland. Irish farmers mark their sheep with spray paint so they can tell which ones are theirs.**

Currency

Ireland is one of seventeen members of the European Union that use the euro as currency. The symbol for the euro is €. One euro is divided into 100 cents. Coins come in values of 1, 2, 5, 10, 20, and 50 cents, plus €1 and €2. Coins are issued by individual countries in the Eurozone. One side of the coin is the same in all countries. It shows a map of Europe. The other side is designed by the country issuing the coins. Ireland puts a harp on all its coins. Euro bills, or banknotes, come in seven different amounts: €5, €10, €20, €50, €100, €200, and €500. They are the same in every Eurozone country. Each denomination is a different color, and each shows examples of a different era of architecture. For example, the €50 shows Renaissance architecture, and the €500 shows modern architecture. In 2013, €1 equaled US$1.34 and €0.75 equaled US$1.

Ireland is used for agriculture. Ireland is still a nation of small farmers. The average farm is about 80 acres (33 hectares) in size.

Beef is the most important agricultural product in Ireland. Ireland is the largest producer of beef in Europe and the fourth largest in the world. Milk and pigs are also important products. Sheep range on hills throughout the country. Grains such as barley and wheat grow well in the east and southeast of Ireland. Other major crops include sugar beets and potatoes.

Mining

Starting as early as 2000 BCE, Ireland was a source of copper for Europe. It also provided gold and silver. It even had a gold rush at the start of the nineteenth century.

Today, the major minerals found in Ireland are zinc and lead, which usually occur together. Ireland is the largest producer of zinc in Europe and the second-largest producer of lead. Barite and gypsum are also mined in Ireland. Barite has many uses, but the main one is in oil drilling. Gypsum is used in drywall for construction. Ireland's mines and quarries also provide crushed stone for roads and buildings. They supplied a huge amount of concrete to the United Kingdom for buildings constructed for the 2012 London Olympics.

Manufacturing

Many different kinds of products are made in Ireland. Chemicals and electrical equipment are among the most valuable. Food and beverages are also important to the manufacturing sector. Guinness beer has been brewed in Dublin since 1759. In recent years, many small brewers, called craft brewers, have emerged in Ireland.

The American company Johnson & Johnson has a plant in Limerick that is one of the biggest plants in the world for making contact lenses.

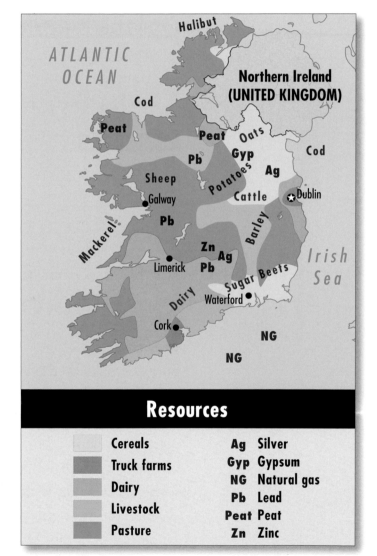

Resources

	Cereals	Ag	Silver
	Truck farms	Gyp	Gypsum
	Dairy	NG	Natural gas
	Livestock	Pb	Lead
	Pasture	Peat	Peat
		Zn	Zinc

What Ireland Grows, Makes, and Mines

AGRICULTURE (2011)

Cow's milk (2009)	5,147,000 metric tons
Barley (2009)	1,167,000 metric tons
Beef (2011)	548,000 metric tons

MANUFACTURING (VALUE OF EXPORTS, 2010)

Medicines	US$35,000,000,000
Computer chips	US$14,000,000,000
Food and beverage products	US$6,000,000,000

MINING (2010)

Gypsum	300,000 metric tons
Zinc	175,000 metric tons
Lead	25,000 metric tons

Another American company, Intel, has been making microchips in county Kildare since the 1980s.

Services

Services make up the largest part of the Irish economy. Services include health care, education, banking, and much more. Tourism is one of the largest parts of the service sector. People come to Ireland from all over the world to explore the ruins of monasteries, listen to fantastic music, and gaze at stunning scenery. Thousands of Irish people work in industries that enable visitors to enjoy their time in Ireland. They work in restaurants and hotels. Some drive taxis, while others sell tickets.

Ireland in Movies

Many people picture Ireland as it appears in the 1952 film *The Quiet Man* (below), which starred John Wayne and Irish-born actress Maureen O'Hara. But that Ireland disappeared long ago. However, films are still being made in Ireland. The Irish Film Board works to make sure that many films and TV shows are made in Ireland.

The government of Ireland provides tax breaks to encourage film production companies to work in Ireland. Ireland also has facilities that make it a good place for television programs and films to be produced.

Ardmore Studios is owned by Paul McGuinness, manager of the rock group U2. Another new studio, called Ashford, was built in Ballyhenry in county Wicklow. It has a main stage that spreads over 30,000 square feet (2,800 square meters). It is surrounded by 300 acres (120 ha) of countryside suitable for backgrounds in many different films. *Vikings* (above), on the History Channel, was filmed at Ashford, but outdoor scenes with Viking longships were filmed at Luggala, an estate in the Wicklow Mountains. Ireland's scenic castles and countryside are also frequently used in films. Large sections of movies such as *Braveheart* and *Saving Private Ryan* were filmed in Ireland.

There are many other kinds of service jobs in Ireland as well. Many are in the information and technology industries. The new international headquarters of LinkedIn, a huge professional network, and the European headquarters of Google, Paypal, and Facebook are all in Dublin. Dropbox, an American cloud-storage firm for sharing files, is opening an operation center in Dublin to serve the tens of millions of Dropbox customers in Europe.

CHAPTER 7

The People of Ireland

I N 2011, THE REPUBLIC OF IRELAND HAD A POPULATION of 4,588,252. That is at least two million people fewer than lived in Ireland before the Great Famine of the nineteenth century. Today, about 60 percent of the population lives in cities. The other 40 percent lives in rural areas. This makes it one of the most rural countries in western Europe.

Opposite: **People walk across the Ha'penny Bridge in Dublin. The bridge, which is only for pedestrians, was built in 1816 and is a symbol of the city.**

Language

Irish is the first official language of Ireland, even though a much smaller percentage of the people speak it than speak English. The name of the language in Irish is Gaeilge, and the language is also called Irish Gaelic. There is also a Scottish Gaelic and the Gaelic used on the Isle of Man.

After the English invaded Ireland, English became the language of business and government in Ireland. But in rural areas and among the poor, Irish continued to be the dominant language into the nineteenth century. In some areas

Populations of Largest Cities (2011)	
Dublin	1,110,627
Cork	198,582
Limerick	91,454
Galway	76,778
Waterford	51,519

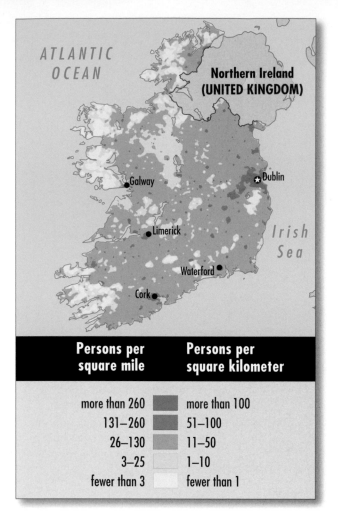

ATLANTIC
OCEAN

Northern Ireland
(UNITED KINGDOM)

Galway

Dublin

Limerick

*Irish
Sea*

Waterford

Cork

Persons per square mile	Persons per square kilometer
more than 260	more than 100
131–260	51–100
26–130	11–50
3–25	1–10
fewer than 3	fewer than 1

of the country, Irish was never wiped out. The areas of Ireland where Irish is the most common spoken language are called Gaeltacht districts. The largest Gaeltacht districts are in counties Donegal and Galway, but other counties in the west also have them.

In 2011, about one hundred thousand people said that Irish was their first language in daily life. This number is increasing. Almost 42 percent of the population can speak Irish.

The Irish government produces an Irish-language television channel called TG4. It broadcasts about seven hours of Irish programming each day, along with English- and French-language programs.

Choose Your Irish

There are three main dialects, or versions, of Irish. One is from Munster, the southwest region of the country. Another is from Connacht, the western region of the country, and the third is from Ulster, the northern region of the country. Munster Irish is the most common. Here is an example of how the dialects differ. Each sentence below says "How are you?"

Munster: *Conas atá tú?*

Connacht: *Cén chaoi a bhfuil tú?*

Ulster: *Cad é mar a tá tú?*

Irish is considered one of the hardest languages to learn. It does not use the letters *j, k, q, w, x, y,* or *z,* but each of the consonants can be pronounced in more than one way. It also has accents applied to vowels. The accent makes the vowel sound longer than it would normally be.

The Family

In 1965, the average woman in Ireland had four children. Today, that average has dropped to two. That is enough children to replace the father and mother and keep the population stable, not taking into account people moving into or out of Ireland.

Gaeltacht Areas

Gaeltacht areas

The Catholic Church does not approve of divorce, so for many decades it was illegal in Ireland. The constitution banned it. But in 1995, the Irish people voted to amend their constitution and allow divorce. The vote was close, 50.3 percent to 49.7 percent. Irish couples must live apart for five years before they are granted a divorce. Today, nearly 10 percent of Irish people have been divorced.

More and more families are made up of couples who are not married. Some have children. About 87 percent of single-parent families are headed by women. Almost 60 percent of single mothers were working in 2011.

Irish Slang

bog	toilet, also countryside to a city dweller
craic	fun time, especially talking (pronounced *KRAK*)
culchie	a city dweller's name for a country dweller (short for *agriculture*)
Dublin 4	an upper-class person, because it is the postal code for the luxurious section of Dublin
gank	disgusting
Jackeen	a person who lives in Dublin, to someone who lives outside the city
piped telly	cable television

Who Are the Irish?

Over the course of thousands of years, Ireland was invaded and settled by many groups. Today's Irish people are a mix of Celtic, Viking, Norman, and British heritage.

About one in five people in Ireland is under age fifteen.

Polish women make dumplings at a restaurant in Dublin.

In recent decades, many immigrants have moved to Ireland. During the years when the Irish economy was booming, many people moved to Ireland in search of work. In 2011, there were people of 196 different nationalities living there. About 17 percent of the population was foreign born. Ireland's fastest-growing group of immigrants is from eastern Europe, primarily Poland. The number of Poles in Ireland grew from just a few thousand in 2001 to 66,300 in 2006 to 122,600 in 2011. Large numbers of immigrants also came from Slovakia, Lithuania, and Latvia.

In addition to the European immigrants, it is estimated that eighty thousand Chinese people live in Ireland. It is believed that Mandarin Chinese is the third most-spoken language in the country.

Dancers perform at a Chinese New Year festival in Dublin. Dublin has the largest Chinese population in Ireland.

Ethnic Ireland (2011)

White Irish	85.8%
Irish Travellers	0.6%
Other white	9.3%
African	1.3%
Chinese	0.4%
Non-Chinese Asian	1.5%
Mixed and other	0.9%
Not stated	0.2%

One out of every four people in the city of Galway was born outside of Ireland. That makes the little city on the west coast the most culturally diverse city in Ireland. Forty-two percent of the people in the small town of Ballyhaunis in county Mayo are not Irish. They represent at least forty-one different nationalities. These immigrants work primarily in the food-processing industry. Ballyhaunis has Ireland's only mosque, a Muslim house of worship, outside of Dublin.

The western town of Gort, not far from the Cliffs of Moher, has a population that is almost one-third Brazilian. The first Brazilians moved there to work in a meat-processing plant. Other Brazilians then gathered there. On Sundays, one church has a mass in Portuguese, the language of Brazil. Each

June, the people of Gort hold a festival called Quadrilha, which focuses on a traditional Brazilian dance. Irish and Brazilian flags hang together at the festival.

In 2011, 65,078 people of African descent lived in Ireland. In 2007, Rotimi Adebari, a native of Nigeria, was elected the first black mayor of an Irish town, Portlaoise. He had been in Ireland since 2000.

People from Gambia attend an Africa Day event in Dublin. Many Africans immigrated to Ireland during the Celtic Tiger boom.

The Travellers

Irish Travellers, or Pavee, are a small ethnic group that has been a separate part of Ireland's population for at least a thousand years. By tradition, they live nomadic lives. They are often called Gypsies, but the Gypsies are a separate group on the European continent. It is estimated that about thirty-six thousand Travellers live in the republic, and another four thousand live in Northern Ireland.

Travellers generally speak English, though they often use their own language, called Cant or Shelta. A large number of them live in wagons or mobile homes, though that number is dropping as they buy permanent homes. They often breed and sell dogs and horses to earn money. This means that they show up at many fairs to sell their animals. There has often been a lot of prejudice against Travellers, especially when they settle their caravans on private lands without permission.

Leaving and Returning

Ireland has faced hard times throughout its history. When hunger, poverty, or lack of opportunity become too great, Irish people leave, hoping to make a better life elsewhere. After the recent economic problems, many young people saw no chance of getting a job. By 2012, three thousand people were leaving Ireland each month—more than have left Ireland at any time since the Great Famine more than 150 years earlier.

But Irish people also come home. Many Irish people who move to other countries plan to be there only three to five years. This is called midterm emigration. According to the

2011 Irish census, more than half a million Irish nationals had lived elsewhere for at least a year. The number of Irish people who return home varies year by year with the economy. In 2013, the Irish held the Gathering, a yearlong festival to encourage people of Irish heritage to visit Ireland.

Irish children perform at a New Year's Eve ceremony to kick off the Gathering.

CHAPTER 8

Myth and Faith

LONG AGO, THE PEOPLE WHO INHABITED THE ISLAND of Ireland believed that Ireland itself was a goddess and that the land was sacred. The goddess had several names, including Banba, Fódla, and Ériu. The Gaelic name of Ireland, Éire, is from Ériu.

Myth is mixed in with early Irish history. Through the ages, people have told stories to explain people, places, and events. The same object or bit of history may have many different stories.

Mythological Ireland

The mythology of Ireland holds that five races of gods came to the island in ancient times. One group was the Fir Bolg, sometimes called bear people, who started the tradition of high kings who ruled over many tribes. This group was followed by the Tuatha Dé Danann, meaning "peoples of the goddess Danu." They brought the idea of a religion overseen by priests called druids. Some Irish say the Tuatha Dé Danann were defeated

Opposite: **Ireland is known for its medieval high crosses. One of the finest, Muiredach's High Cross, was sculpted in the ninth or tenth century. It is about 19 feet (6 m) high and is covered with religious scenes and geometric decorations.**

According to Irish legend, Eithne (left) was a member of a semi-divine people called the Fomorians. She fell in love with Cian (right), the leader of the Tuatha Dé Danann.

by the next invaders, the Milesians from Iberia (the Spanish peninsula) in a great battle that took place in county Kerry. Defeated, the Tuatha Dé Danann agreed to move underground. Legend has it they may have turned into fairies.

Many mythological creatures of Ireland come from the tales of the Tuatha Dé Danann. The Otherworld, the land of the spirits, is occupied by such beings as fairies, sprites, leprechauns (a type of fairy known for hoarding gold), and banshees, female spirits who warn of death to come. Their world intertwines with the human world on occasion, such as when hobgoblins or brownies do small chores. But these beings can also do mischief, such as making a cow stop giving milk.

Ancient stories often define places in Ireland today. Mermaids and mermen are said to occupy the caves along the western cliffs. A highway being built between Galway and the Shannon Airport during the Celtic Tiger days inspired protests from lovers of Ireland's folktales, because it would have plowed through an area where sprites were said to meet. After the protests, the government built the road around the large hawthorn bush believed to be the meeting place.

The Druids

The religious leaders of Ireland in the years before Christianity were called druids. Very little is known about what they

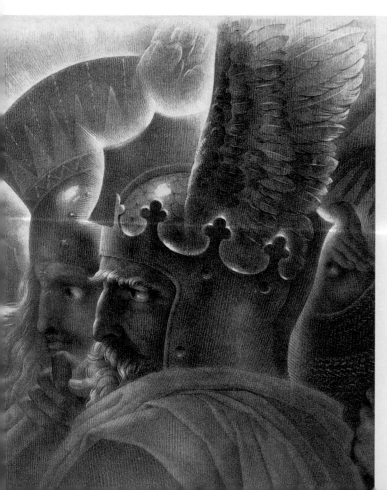

Warrior Tales

Stories of individuals, perhaps human, perhaps super-human, are an important part of Irish myth. Finn McCool (Fionn mac Cumhaill in Irish) was a wise and strong—and possibly gigantic—legendary hero said to have lived in county Kildare. In the nineteenth century, the Irish fighting for independence from Great Britain were often called Fenians, and they took their name from Finn. The story goes that Finn created the rugged landscape called the Burren. The great dome of limestone rock was created when Finn McCool and a rival tossed a boulder back and forth during a battle.

The giant Cuhullin (or Cú Chulainn) took on Finn McCool. Finn bit off Cuhullin's middle finger, which was where Cuhullin's power was stored, and so was able to defeat him. A statue of dead Cuhullin commemorates the 1916 Easter Rising in the Dublin General Post Office.

Druids cut sprigs of mistletoe, a plant that often grows high in trees.

believed. They supposedly served as messengers between this world and the next. They regarded the oak tree and mistletoe as sacred, and they celebrated the seasons. These facts are why people today think of druidism as a form of nature worship. But in Irish mythology, the druids were sorcerers who could cast both helpful and harmful spells.

The Roman Catholic Church

St. Patrick spread Christianity in Ireland in the 400s. According to legend, he established the first Christian church in Ireland on the Hill of Tara, where the high kings were crowned. Most people on the island soon adopted the religion. Beginning in the 1500s, the English who ruled Ireland tried to suppress Catholicism there. They wanted the Irish to adopt Protestantism. They had little success, though, and Ireland remained overwhelmingly Catholic.

Ireland was an extremely religious country throughout the nineteenth and most of the twentieth centuries. So many churches were built there that anyone anywhere in Ireland could walk to a church, and there were enough priests to run them all. In rural areas, in particular, each parish (an area run by one church) ran most of the activities in town, including the events of sports teams and women's organizations. The local priest had a great deal of authority over the people's lives.

Interest in the priesthood declined in the second half of the twentieth century. Many people had lost interest in religion.

Patron Saints

Patron saints are people who probably lived once but who are thought to still be able to affect people's lives. Ireland has three patron saints. The first is St. Patrick, who helped convert Ireland to Christianity.

The second, St. Brigit of Kildare, lived from about 451 to 523. She was probably born a slave, and was considered holy from birth. As an adult, she founded several monasteries, including one for women. Several miracles were attributed to her. Brigit's cross is an important Irish symbol. Traditionally, women wove these crosses out of plants and hung them in their houses to protect the homes from fire.

The third is St. Columba (near right), or Colum Cille in Irish, which means "dove of the church." He was born in county Donegal in 521 and founded a monastery in the city of Derry, in what is now Northern Ireland. He is known for his prophecies, visions, and miracles. He lived most of his life on the Scottish island of Iona, dying in 597.

Others disliked that the Roman Catholic Church does not allow priests to marry. And as Ireland grew wealthier, many people preferred to go into other professions. Now Ireland has a shortage of priests. By 2000, there were only two seminaries—colleges for the priesthood—left in Ireland. Many people entering a seminary today are older. They have already had a career and perhaps been married.

In 1937, Ireland's leader, Éamon de Valera, and his advisers, who were mostly officials in the Catholic Church, wrote into the nation's new constitution that the Catholic Church had a "special position" in Ireland because it was the church of most of the people. The constitution also guaranteed religious freedom for all Irish citizens.

But the Catholic Church's "special position" gave it great control in Irish society. For example, a ban on divorce was written into the constitution.

In the eighteenth century, the church began setting up Magdalene asylums. Run by nuns, these were places unmarried mothers, girls whose parents thought they were too much trouble, and other women could be sent, supposedly

Most Irish schools include religious instruction.

for their own safety. In the asylums, the young women usually did laundry. They were supposed to stay only until they were twenty-one years old, but some Irish women were never told they could leave. They stayed, virtually as slaves, for a lifetime. Similarly, boys could be sent to industrial schools, which were also supervised by the church. The children were often abused. These institutions were gradually closed in the second half of the twentieth century, and in 1999, the taoiseach apologized to all Irish people who had been mistreated under this system.

Survivors of the Magdalene laundries leave following an apology from the taoiseach. An estimated thirty thousand women were sent to Magdalene laundries in Ireland.

Over the years, many people came to believe that the church's influence was holding Ireland back from becoming a modern nation. In 1972, the constitution was amended to remove mention of the Roman Catholic Church's "special position." More than 80 percent of voters approved of this, and Éamon de Valera signed it into law. Politicians began criticizing the church openly, something they had only rarely done before.

In 1973, 91 percent of Catholics in Ireland attended church every week. Recent surveys have shown that this has dropped significantly. About 35 percent of Catholics now attend church weekly. That is still a higher rate of attendance than in any other western European country.

Irish people attend mass in Clifden, a town in the west of Ireland. People in rural Ireland are twice as likely to attend mass regularly as people in Irish cities.

St. Patrick's Cathedral, an Anglican church in Dublin, is the largest church in Ireland.

Religion in Ireland (2011)

Roman Catholic	84.2%
Church of Ireland	2.8%
Orthodox	1.0%
Other Christian	2.5%
Islam	1.1%
Other non-Christian	0.8%
No religion	5.9%
No answer	1.6%

Note: Does not equal 100% because of rounding

Other Religions

In the 1530s, King Henry VIII made England into a Protestant country, and the English Catholic Church became the Church of England, also known as the Anglican Church. The beliefs of Anglicans and Catholics are very similar, but Anglicans do not regard the pope as the head of the church. The Church of Ireland is the Irish version of the Church of England. It is the largest Protestant church in Ireland, but less than 3 percent of the Irish worship in it.

Other Protestant churches that are active in Ireland include Methodist, Presbyterian, Baptist, Pentecostal, and Assemblies of God. However, in 2011, worshippers in these churches made up little more than 5 percent of the population. The number of people claiming "no religion" is larger.

Muslims first came to Ireland in the 1950s. Most were students who had gone to Ireland to study. They worshipped in their homes because they didn't have their own houses of worship. The first mosque (Islamic house of worship) in Ireland was opened in Dublin in 1976. Today, about fifty thousand Muslims live in Ireland. Most are of Asian or African origin. There are nine mosques or Islamic cultural centers in the republic.

There has been a small but active Jewish presence in Ireland for a thousand years or more. Today, there are fewer than two thousand Jews in Ireland. There are four synagogues (Jewish houses of worship) in Ireland, three in Dublin, and one in Cork.

A mother and child in suburban Dublin prepare to go to a feast marking the end of Ramadan, the holiest time in the Muslim calendar. Many Irish Muslims are immigrants from Asia or Africa.

CHAPTER 9

Music, Literature, and Sports

MUSIC HAS A RICH TRADITION IN IRELAND, AND as Irish people moved to other countries that tradition was exported. Traditional Irish music played an important role in the development of American folk and country music.

Traditional Instruments

The Irish harp is a symbol of Ireland, but it is not played very often. Smaller than the harps seen in symphony orchestras, Irish harps have existed since at least medieval times. Harpers used to be important figures in courts and the homes of the wealthy, where they played music and told stories.

Irish bagpipes are called *uilleann* (pronounced ILL-un) pipes. They are usually played along with fiddles and whistles. The Irish drum, called a *bodhrán* (BOWR-ahn), was originally used in battle, but now it is a performance instrument. It has been described as being the "heartbeat" of Irish music.

In the 1960s, a Dublin band called the Chieftains introduced these traditional instruments to a wider audience. The group has been playing ever since.

The Chieftains is primarily an instrumental group. The band was central in the surge in popularity of Irish music around the world that began in the 1970s.

Music and Dance

Irish folk music was made popular by bands such as Clannad, the Clancy Brothers, and the Dubliners. They raised interest in Irish music all over the world. One member of the Clannad family, named Enya, often uses folk melodies in her own writing.

Some Irish singers of classical music have also gained worldwide attention. One of the first was an opera singer named John McCormack. In the early twentieth century, he gained worldwide popularity singing Irish ballads in his rich voice. More recently, PBS television put together a group called the Irish Tenors. The three tenors are currently Anthony Kearns, Ronan Tynan, and Finbar Wright. Their operatic performances of traditional Irish songs have been hugely popular.

Many Irish performers have become successful rock and pop singers. Sinéad O'Connor, who was born in Glenageary, near Dublin, is a rock singer, writer, and instrumentalist who became famous in the late 1980s. Glen Hansard performs with the group the Frames. He also starred in the film *Once*, in which he played a Dublin street musician. He won an Academy Award, or Oscar, for Best Original Song for "Falling Slowly," which appeared in that film. Ronan Keating and his friends formed the group Boyzone, though he also records alone. Other popular Irish groups include the Corrs, the Cranberries, and the Hothouse Flowers.

Glen Hansard and Czech perfomer Markéta Irglová hold the Oscars they won for Best Original Song in 2008.

Bono and U2

The most famous Irish musician is probably Bono, whose real name is Paul Hewson. A native of the Dublin area, Bono has been part of the group U2 since it was formed in 1976, when its members were still in high school. Bono writes most of the group's lyrics, which range from rebellious to religious. He has long been an activist on issues such as peace and helping poor countries.

After nearly forty years of playing together, U2 has become one of the most successful bands in history. The band has produced many hit records, including "One" and "I Still Haven't Found What I'm Looking For." As of 2012, U2 had won twenty-two Grammy Awards—more than any other band. The group was inducted into the Rock and Roll Hall of Fame in 2005.

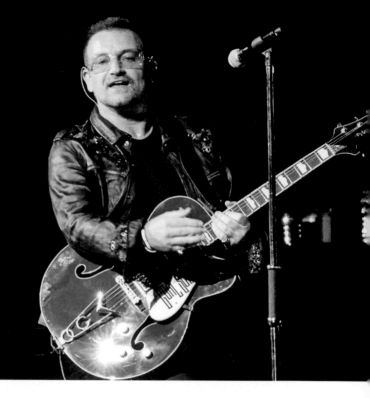

Traditional Irish music was played at dances, and Ireland still has a strong tradition of folk dancing. This kind of dance sometimes includes rousing, foot-stamping jigs. Irish step dancing is also popular. Performed to lively music, it features rapid foot and leg movements, while the upper body and arms remain motionless. In the 1990s, the Irish dance troupe Riverdance raised the profile of Irish step dancing in the United States and around the world. They performed for months in London, New York, and other cities.

Literature

Ireland has an extraordinarily rich literary tradition. William Butler Yeats (1865–1939) is considered one of the greatest poets of the twentieth century. Yeats and playwright Augusta, Lady Gregory founded the Abbey Theatre, Ireland's national theater, in 1904, when they converted an old morgue into a theater. That building burned down in 1951, but a new one quickly took its place. It is still the center of Irish drama.

John Millington Synge's playwriting career lasted only six years, but in those few years he created some of Ireland's greatest plays, including *The Playboy of the Western World*, *Riders to the Sea*, and *The Aran Islands*, which portrayed the harsh life in western Ireland. His plays were performed—not always to acclaim—in the Abbey Theatre. Sean O'Casey followed Synge as the main contributor to the Abbey. He is most famous for *The Plough and the Stars* and *Juno and the Paycock*, about working-class families in Dublin.

Guinness Begins Record Books

One of the most famous books to come out of Ireland is *The Guinness Book of Records*. The idea for the book began on a hunting expedition in county Wexford in 1951, when Hugh Beaver, the director of Guinness Breweries, got into an argument with other hunters over what was the fastest game bird. The first *Guinness Book of Records* was published in 1955, and it immediately became a best seller. Since 2000, it has been known as *Guinness World Records*. All kinds of facts can be found in the book: The world's tallest dog (left) measures 7 feet 4 inches (2.2 m) when standing on his hind legs. The youngest person to visit every country in the world is an Italian named Maurizio Giuliano, who completed the task at age twenty-eight. And on March 25, 2011, in county Clare, Ireland, Fiona Nolan wore the most socks ever on one foot—152!

Several of Ireland's greatest writers have been awarded the Nobel Prize in Literature, the world's highest literary honor. Yeats was the first Irish person to win this prize, in 1923. The committee that chose him said his poetry gave "expression to the spirit of a whole nation." Two years later, playwright George

George Bernard Shaw at work at his home in 1946. He wrote more than sixty plays during his career.

Bernard Shaw won the award. Shaw's plays are still frequently performed. He is best known for his play *Pygmalion*, which became the musical *My Fair Lady*. In 1969, the prize went to another playwright, Samuel Beckett. His work is considered absurdist, and focuses on the essence of human life and misery. His best-known play, *Waiting for Godot*, concerns two miserable men who don't know why they are where they are. They are waiting for a mysterious man named Godot who never shows up. In 1995, the Nobel Prize went to another poet, Seamus Heaney. Heaney turned the medieval epic *Beowulf* into modern English poetry.

Oscar Wilde is remembered for his sharp wit, both in his work and in his life.

Oscar Wilde never won a Nobel Prize, but his works endure. There are many different film versions of his very funny play *The Importance of Being Earnest*, and the play is still performed in theaters today. Wilde's novel, *The Picture of Dorian Gray*, about a man who does not age but whose portrait does, sends chills up the spine.

Say the name Dublin to serious readers and they quickly think of James Joyce (1882–1941). He created a character named Leopold Bloom, who was at the center of the novel *Ulysses*, which takes place in one day in Dublin. It is a complex novel that portrays the characters' thoughts in all their

Ulysses **is set on June 16. Every year on that day, some people in Dublin celebrate James Joyce and his masterful novel by dressing up in costume and retracing the steps of the book's characters.**

jumbled, random patterns. *Ulysses* is often regarded as the most important novel in the English language.

Another Dubliner named Bram Stoker wrote *Dracula*, one of the best-selling novels of all time. The name of his vampire comes from an Irish phrase, *droch ola*, which means "bad blood." This novel is the source of most of the vampire tales of today.

Sports

Versions of soccer, called football in Ireland, were played in Ireland in medieval times when groups of boys got together to play with a ball. The modern game was brought to Ireland from England in the eighteenth century. League of Ireland is the country's major soccer league. It has nineteen clubs. The most successful team in the league is Shamrock Rovers of Dublin.

Gaelic football is a game unique to Ireland. In this game, two teams of fifteen players each can do just about anything with the round ball to get it down the field and through the

Gaelic football is the most popular sport in Ireland in terms of attendance. Some matches draw more than eighty thousand fans.

goal posts. The Gaelic Athletic Association (GAA) also covers the Irish games of men's hurling and women's camogie. Both games are a little like field hockey. Players use a stick to move the ball. The GAA also wrote rules for rounders, the game that many think is the ancestor of baseball.

On the Water

Ireland has a long coastline, and some people take advantage of it to play water sports. Lahinch Beach is a popular surfing site, with waves that may reach 25 feet (7.6 m). Some adventurous people surf near the Cliffs of Moher. One of the centers of water sports in Ireland is Lough Hyne in West Cork. Snorkeling, diving, surfing, and kayaking are all popular there.

Katie Taylor, Boxing Champ

Since Ireland became independent, Irish athletes have won nine gold medals at the Olympics, all in the summer games. Swimmer Michelle Smith won three gold medals in 1996. Ireland did not win another gold medal until 2012, when Katie Taylor (in red) took home the gold in the women's lightweight division in boxing. It was the first time that women's boxing had been included in the games. Raised in Bray, a town south of Dublin, Taylor began boxing at age twelve, and her father, who was an amateur boxer, is her coach. She won the world championship in her weight class the first time in 2008. Taylor has helped make women's boxing more popular in Ireland and around the world. She also plays soccer and Gaelic football.

A man fishes for salmon in county Kerry.

Fishing is also popular in Ireland. People in Ireland take to the nation's many rivers and lakes in hopes of catching bream, perch, dace, and other species. Ireland is also a popular destination for game fishing. People come from all over the world to try to catch salmon and sea trout. Any river that empties into the sea is a good place to try for these big fish. The River Moy in county Sligo is the most popular place in Ireland to fish for Atlantic salmon. It is estimated that seventy-five thousand salmon return to the river each spring and summer.

The Irish Grand National is a steeplechase race. The horses must jump over fences and ditches.

Horse Racing

Horse racing is one of the most popular pastimes in Ireland. Flat racing, steeplechase (a race over long distances with hurdles), and hunting are all popular with riders and audiences. Household names include those of jockeys and trainers, as well as the most successful horses. Tracks are located all over the country. Horses that have been bred and trained in Ireland have often raced in the Kentucky Derby and other American flat races.

The Irish National Stud is a renowned horse-breeding program. It has been located on a farm in Tully, in county Kildare, since 1917, when the owner donated it to the nation. The farm continues to produce champion horses. The museum at the Stud features the skeleton of Arkle, voted the most popular racehorse of all time in Britain and Ireland. He died in 1970.

Several types of horses are particularly associated with Ireland. Irish breeders developed a breed called the Irish sport horse, which is often used for fox hunting and show jumping. The Connemara pony is an older breed that may have developed from Scandinavian horses brought to Ireland by Vikings. Clifden, in county Galway, holds a huge international Connemara pony show every year.

Connemara ponies are calm, strong, and hardy.

CHAPTER 10

Food, School, and Fun

IT IS SAID THAT THE POTATO WAS BROUGHT TO IRELAND by Sir Walter Raleigh, a wealthy Englishman who planted the crop on his estate near Cork before 1600. The old laws set down by the English required meat and grains grown in Ireland to go to England, or at least to the cities of Ireland. That left the rural poor of Ireland to survive on potatoes, with perhaps some herring and milk. Fortunately, the food was healthy enough for them to live on. It is estimated that before the Great Famine, an adult in Ireland ate about 10 pounds (4.5 kg) of potatoes each day.

Opposite: **Many Irish towns, including Galway, are filled with brightly painted buildings.**

Irish Food

Some of the best-known Irish foods involve potatoes. Boxty is a potato pancake whose Irish name means "poorhouse bread." Also known as poundy, it is made from grated potato mixed with a little flour and sometimes egg to hold it together. Then it is fried. If made thin enough, it can be used to make a wrap for meat or vegetables. If it has sugar and cream added, it becomes a sweet treat called stampy.

It was reported in 2011 that the potato was falling in popularity as the main starch for dinner in Ireland. Couscous, rice, pasta, and noodles were replacing it. Paula Mee, a nutritionist, said, "There is a legacy attached to the potato, and it obviously isn't a happy one. It is in our DNA to regard the potato as a peasant food linked to a past we would obviously all rather leave behind us."

Irish breakfasts often include bread, fruit, and tea.

Colcannon Traditions

Colcannon is a typical Irish dish of mashed potatoes mixed with kale or cabbage. Traditionally, when making this dish for a gathering, the cook would hide a ring and a coin in the colcannon. The dish was passed around, with each person taking a spoonful. The person who got the ring was said to be the next to marry. The person who found the coin would come into a fortune. Test your luck with this recipe, and have an adult help you.

Ingredients

6 large potatoes

1 bunch of kale

½ stick of butter, melted

½ cup milk

6 scallions

Salt and pepper

1 tablespoon chopped parsley

Directions

Peel the potatoes and cut them into large pieces. Boil water and cook the potatoes in it until they are soft. This usually takes about 10 minutes. Mash the potatoes. Take the kale leaves off the large stems and chop them into small pieces. Boil the kale leaves until soft, about 20 minutes. Drain the kale and mix it with half the butter. Put the milk in a small saucepan. Chop the scallions and add them to the milk. Add salt and pepper to taste. Bring this mixture to a boil. Mix together the mashed potatoes, the kale, and the boiling milk. Mix until light and fluffy. Stir in the remaining butter and sprinkle the parsley on top. Enjoy!

The Shamrock Chinese takeaway restaurant is in Donegal Town, in northwestern Ireland. Takeaway is what Americans call takeout.

Virtually any meal in Ireland can be accompanied by soda bread. Unlike yeast bread, which requires time to rise before baking, soda bread can be shaped in a pan and baked quickly. A popular bread using yeast is barmbrack, which means "speckled loaf." Its name comes from the fact that it has raisins in it.

In recent years, many immigrants have moved to Ireland, bringing the foods of their home countries with them. Irish food now includes foods from all around the world. Every city and many small towns have restaurants featuring foods from Japan, India, China, Afghanistan, and South America.

Education

In Ireland, all children must go to school between the ages of six and sixteen, or complete at least three years of high school. Since 2010, preschool has been offered free for one year before the start of primary school.

Irish children study all the usual subjects, including math, language, science, history, and art. Children are also taught the Irish language. The school day typically runs from 9:00 a.m. to 3:00 p.m. In high school, it often runs until 4:00 p.m. The school year lasts from September until June, and summer vacation is July and August.

Irish schoolchildren take part in a soccer match. Some Irish children play sports in school, while others play with community or youth groups.

There are four types of primary schools. Most children attend national schools. These are government-funded and are partially under the control of a religious institution. Religion is taught at these schools. Most national schools are Roman Catholic, but there are also Church of Ireland, Presbyterian, and multidenominational national schools. Ireland also has one Jewish and two Muslim national schools.

The next most common type of primary school is a Gaelscoil, a school in which all of the classes are taught using the Irish language. About 10 percent of students go to Gaelscoils. They are the fastest-growing type of school and can

Some Irish schools require children to wear uniforms, but many schools do not.

The Scoil Choilm
Community National
School in Dublin serves
children of all religions.

be found all around the country. Multidenominational schools are also growing in popularity. These are schools that are open to students of all religious backgrounds. Preparatory schools are the final type of primary school. These are private schools that charge fees and do not rely on government funding.

There are several types of secondary schools. Those called voluntary schools are the general public schools, though churches or other groups manage them. More than half of all students attend these. The rest go to state-run vocational schools or community schools, which are a combination of both types. About 3 percent of the population attends Irish-speaking secondary schools. At the end of secondary school, students must pass a Leaving Certificate Examination.

About ninety thousand students are attending university in Ireland at any given time.

Colleges and Universities

College education is free for everyone in Ireland and for students from elsewhere in the European Union. There are service fees, however, which amount almost to a tuition fee. The best-educated groups in Ireland are people who are in their twenties and thirties. They have completed more full-time education than any previous generation, and many more women than men have completed college.

Ireland's oldest university is Trinity College in Dublin. It was founded in 1592. For a long time, it was regarded as the university of the Protestant Ascendancy only. Catholic bishops banned Catholic students from attending it until 1972. Oscar Wilde and George Bernard Shaw went to Trinity.

University College is the national university with campuses in Dublin, Galway, and Cork. Founded in 1854, it is now Ireland's largest university.

Trinity College Library is the largest research library in Ireland, housing about five million books. Its Old Library displays the Book of Kells and other magnificent manuscripts.

Public Holidays

New Year's Day	January 1
St. Patrick's Day	March 17
Easter Monday	March or April
May Day	First Monday in May
June holiday	First Monday in June
August holiday	First Monday in August
October holiday	Last Monday in October
All Saints' Day	November 1
Immaculate Conception	December 8
Christmas Day	December 25
St. Stephen's Day	December 26

The National University of Ireland (NUI) is really a system of schools, with headquarters in Dublin. It includes general universities as well as specialized schools such as the National College of Art and Design and the Royal College of Surgeons in Ireland.

Holidays

The spirits seem to come alive at Halloween, a holiday that began in Ireland. Halloween began as Samhain, one of the four major festivals in ancient Ireland. But in the seventh century, the pope wanted people to stop celebrating a pagan, or pre-Christian, holiday, and he introduced All Hallows' Day, or All Saints' Day on November 1. The night before became a special time called Hallows' Eve, or Halloween, when banshees and other spirits would be at work.

The tradition of trick-or-treating may date back to pre-Christian Ireland. At that time, it was the custom of the druids, the priests of the time, to collect nuts, apples, and perhaps eggs from each home. If people didn't give the druids enough treats, the druids might play tricks on them. It is said that the druids would disguise themselves in costumes to keep the evil spirits away. On Samhain, early Irish people also hollowed out turnips, carved faces in them, and put a candle inside. This figure came to be called Stingy Jack, or Jack O'Lantern, who was able to trick the devil.

A blue witch joins a Halloween celebration in Dublin.

Henry Street in Dublin is bright with decorations during the Christmas season.

Christmas is the biggest holiday in Ireland. People decorate their homes with Christmas trees and scenes of Jesus's birth. Many more people than average attend mass on Christmas Eve and Christmas Day. Mumming is also a Christmas tra-

Many people take time during the Christmas season to visit the graves of loved ones.

dition. Mummers are actors who perform traditional plays. Sometimes they perform in streets, walking through towns. Other times they perform in local pubs.

Christmas is also a time to remember dead relatives. Following a Christmas tradition, people decorate graves with wreathes made of holly and ivy. In this country, filled with vivid history and strong traditions, people remember those who have gone before.

Timeline

<table>
<tr><td colspan="2">IRISH HISTORY</td><td colspan="2">WORLD HISTORY</td></tr>
<tr><td>People first arrive in Ireland.</td><td>ca. 6000 BCE</td><td></td><td></td></tr>
<tr><td>Ancient Irish people build great tombs.</td><td>ca. 3200–2500 BCE</td><td>ca. 2500 BCE</td><td>The Egyptians build the pyramids and the Sphinx in Giza.</td></tr>
<tr><td>The first Celtic people arrive from the continent.</td><td>ca. 600 BCE</td><td>ca. 563 BCE</td><td>The Buddha is born in India.</td></tr>
<tr><td>St. Patrick works to convert people to Christianity.</td><td>432–461 CE</td><td>313 CE</td><td>The Roman emperor Constantine legalizes Christianity.</td></tr>
<tr><td>Irish monasteries draw scholars from the continent.</td><td>ca. 500</td><td>610</td><td>The Prophet Muhammad begins preaching a new religion called Islam.</td></tr>
<tr><td>Vikings gain control of Ireland.</td><td>795</td><td></td><td></td></tr>
<tr><td>The Book of Kells is created.</td><td>ca. 800</td><td></td><td></td></tr>
<tr><td>Dublin is founded by Vikings.</td><td>841</td><td></td><td></td></tr>
<tr><td>King Brian Boru's forces defeat Vikings in the Battle of Clontarf.</td><td>1014</td><td>1054</td><td>The Eastern (Orthodox) and Western (Roman Catholic) Churches break apart.</td></tr>
<tr><td></td><td></td><td>1095</td><td>The Crusades begin.</td></tr>
<tr><td>England takes control of Ireland.</td><td>1155</td><td>1215</td><td>King John seals the Magna Carta.</td></tr>
<tr><td>The Irish create a parliament.</td><td>1297</td><td>1300s</td><td>The Renaissance begins in Italy.</td></tr>
<tr><td></td><td></td><td>1347</td><td>The plague sweeps through Europe.</td></tr>
<tr><td></td><td></td><td>1453</td><td>Ottoman Turks capture Constantinople, conquering the Byzantine Empire.</td></tr>
<tr><td></td><td></td><td>1492</td><td>Columbus arrives in North America.</td></tr>
<tr><td>Henry VIII of England is named king of Ireland; he tries to establish Protestantism there.</td><td>1541</td><td>1500s</td><td>Reformers break away from the Catholic Church, and Protestantism is born.</td></tr>
<tr><td>Scots settlers are given land in northern Ireland.</td><td>Early 1600s</td><td></td><td></td></tr>
<tr><td>The Protestant Ascendancy rules Ireland.</td><td>Late 1600s–1700s</td><td>1776</td><td>The U.S. Declaration of Independence is signed.</td></tr>
</table>

IRISH HISTORY

The Act of Union joins England, Scotland, Wales, and Ireland.	**1801**
One million people die during the Great Famine.	**1845–1849**
The Sinn Féin political party is founded to work toward Irish independence.	**1905**
Irish rebels try to oust the British in the failed Easter Rising.	**1916**
Sinn Féin wins 73 seats in the British Parliament but sets up the Irish Parliament instead.	**1918**
The Irish fight the Anglo-Irish War to achieve independence.	**1919–1921**
The Irish Free State is established.	**1922**
Ireland declares itself neutral in European wars.	**1937**
The Republic of Ireland Act makes Ireland a republic and eliminates all ties with the United Kingdom.	**1948**
Ireland joins the European Economic Community.	**1973**
The Irish economy begins to boom.	**1995**
Ireland adopts the euro as its currency.	**2002**
The economy suffers a severe downturn.	**2008**
Enda Kenny is elected taoiseach.	**2011**

WORLD HISTORY

1789	The French Revolution begins.
1865	The American Civil War ends.
1879	The first practical lightbulb is invented.
1914	World War I begins.
1917	The Bolshevik Revolution brings communism to Russia.
1929	A worldwide economic depression begins.
1939	World War II begins.
1945	World War II ends.
1969	Humans land on the Moon.
1975	The Vietnam War ends.
1989	The Berlin Wall is torn down as communism crumbles in Eastern Europe.
1991	The Soviet Union breaks into separate states.
2001	Terrorists attack the World Trade Center in New York City and the Pentagon near Washington, D.C.
2004	A tsunami in the Indian Ocean destroys coastlines in Africa, India, and Southeast Asia.
2008	The United States elects its first African American president.

Fast Facts

Official name: Republic of Ireland

Capital: Dublin

Official languages: Irish and English

Dublin

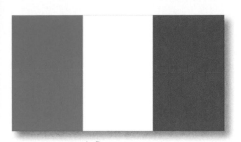

Irish flag

Powerscourt Waterfall

Official religion:	None
Year of founding:	1922 as the Irish Free State, 1948 as the Republic of Ireland
National anthem:	"Amhrán na bhFiann" ("The Soldiers' Song")
Form of government:	Republic
Head of state:	President
Head of government:	Taoiseach (prime minister)
Area of country:	27,133 square miles (70,274 sq km)
Bordering country:	Northern Ireland
Highest elevation:	Carrantuohill, 3,415 feet (1,041 m) above sea level
Lowest elevation:	North Slob, county Wexford, 10 feet (3 m) below sea level
Longest river:	Shannon, 240 miles (386 km)
Largest lake:	Lough Corrib, 69 square miles (179 sq km)
Average daily high temperature:	In Dublin, 48°F (9°C) in January, 68°F (20°C) in July
Average daily low temperature:	In Dublin, 39°F (4°C) in January, 56°F (13°C) in July
Average annual precipitation:	21 inches (53 cm) in Dublin; 48 inches (122 cm) in Cork
Latitude and longitude of geographic center:	10°S, 55°W

Cork

National population (2011 est.):	4,588,252	
Population of major cities (2011 est.):	Dublin	1,110,627
	Cork	198,582
	Limerick	91,454
	Galway	76,778
	Waterford	51,519

Landmarks:
- ▶ *The Burren*, county Clare
- ▶ *Cliffs of Moher*, Doolin
- ▶ *Dublin Castle*, Dublin
- ▶ *Newgrange*, county Meath
- ▶ *Ring of Kerry*, Iveragh Peninsula

Economy: Electronic equipment, medical technology, software, and food and beverages are among the major products made in Ireland. Service industries such as call centers and tourism are important to the nation's economy. Ireland is a major exporter of beef and dairy products. Barley, wheat, sugar beets, and potatoes are also important crops.

Currency: The euro. In 2013, €1 equaled US$1.34 and €0.75 equaled US$1.

System of weights and measures: Metric system

Literacy rate (2011): 99%

Currency

Schoolchildren

Bono

Common Irish words and phrases:		
Tá or Sea		Yes
Níl or Ní hea		No
Dia fhuit		Hello (literally "God be with you")
Slán		Good-bye
Le do thoil		Please
Go raibh maith agat		Thank you
Fir		Men
Mná		Women

Prominent Irish: Bono (Paul Hewson) (1960–)
Member of the rock band U2

Éamon de Valera (1882–1975)
Political leader, founder of Sinn Féin

James Joyce (1882–1941)
Novelist

Daniel O'Connell (1775–1847)
Political leader

Charles Stewart Parnell (1846–1891)
Political leader

George Bernard Shaw (1856–1950)
Nobel Prize–winning playwright

Katie Taylor (1986–)
Olympic champion boxer

William Butler Yeats (1865–1939)
Nobel Prize–winning poet

To Find Out More

Books

▶ Bartoletti, Susan Campbell. *Black Potatoes: The Story of the Great Irish Famine, 1845-1850*. New York: Houghton Mifflin Harcourt, 2005.

▶ Daly, Ita. *Stories from Ireland*. New York: Oxford University Press, 2009.

▶ McDonnell, Vincent. *Ireland: Our Island Story*. Cork, Ireland: Collins Press, 2011.

Music

▶ The Chieftains. *The Essential Chieftains*. New York: RCA, 2006.

▶ *From Galway to Dublin: Early Recordings of Traditional Irish Music*. Burlington, MA: Rounder, 1996.

▶ U2. *U218 Singles*. New York: Interscope, 2006.

▶ **Visit this Scholastic Web site for more information on Ireland:**
www.factsfornow.scholastic.com
Enter the keyword **Ireland**

Index

Page numbers in *italics*
indicate illustrations.

Meet the Author

IRELAND—ITS PEOPLE, ITS FOLKLORE, ITS HISTORY, its land—became a favorite subject for Jean Blashfield from the first time she saw the country. At the time, Ireland was rather isolated and poor, but beautiful nonetheless. She's been amazed and intrigued at the changes that have taken place in Ireland since then. It has turned into an exciting, vibrant, forward-looking country that has accepted the challenges it still has to face.

Blashfield loves Ireland but is also a lover of cats, the Internet, children, the rest of Europe, travel, books, sunshine, and much, much more. Most of all she delights in sharing what she enjoys with other people. One way she does this is by writing books on her favorite subjects. Sometimes, she says, her biggest problem is figuring out what to leave out of a book because she becomes so fascinated by every bit of information. In fact, she's written several books of trivia in which she's collected lots of details that she wasn't able to put into other books!

Blashfield has written more than 160 books, most of them for young people. Many of them have been for Scholastic's Enchantment of the World and America the Beautiful series. She has also created an encyclopedia of aviation and space, written popular books on murderers and houseplants, and had

a lot of fun creating a book on the things women have done, called *Hellraisers, Heroines, and Holy Women.* In addition, she founded the Dungeons & Dragons fantasy book department, which is now part of Hasbro, the big toy and game company.

Born in Madison, Wisconsin, Jean Blashfield grew up in the Chicago area. She graduated from the University of Michigan and worked for publishers in Chicago, New York, and London, and for NASA in Washington, D.C. She returned to Wisconsin when she married Wallace Black (a publisher, writer, and pilot) and began to raise a family. She now has two grown children, one a professor of medieval history and one who manages a department at Stanford University, and three grandchildren.

Photo Credits